Parenting Your Teens and Tweens

with

Grace

Ages 11 – 18

D1224507

Dr. Greg and Lisa Popcak

with Jacob Popcak, MA, and Rachael Isaac, MSW

OSV

Our Sunday Visitor
Huntington, Indiana

Nihil Obstat
Msgr. Michael Heintz, Ph.D.
Censor Librorum

Imprimatur
✠ Kevin C. Rhoades
Bishop of Fort Wayne-South Bend
December 21, 2020

Our Sunday Visitor Publishing Division
Our Sunday Visitor Inc.
200 Noll Plaza
Huntington, IN 46750
www.osv.com
1-800-348-2440

ISBN: 978-1-68192-485-4 (Inventory No. T2376)
1. FAMILY & RELATIONSHIPS—Parenting—General.
2. RELIGION—Christian Life—Family.
3. RELIGION—Christianity—Catholic.

eISBN: 978-1-68192-486-1
LCCN: 2021932401

Cover and interior design: Lindsey Riesen
Cover art: Adobe Stock
Interior art: Jacob Popcak

PRINTED IN THE UNITED STATES OF AMERICA

CONTENTS

Parenting Your
Teens and Tweens with Grace

Introduction

A Letter from the Authors

"The Christian family constitutes a specific revelation and realization of ecclesial communion, and for this reason it can and should be called a domestic church."

Catechism of the Catholic Church 2204

"Why don't teens (and preteens) come with an instruction manual?" They do! But we like to say that the manual is written in "Catholic."

When we began drafting the first edition of *Parenting with Grace* in 2000, we started with a provocative idea. What if, instead of starting with any prior existing assumptions about the "correct" approach to parenting, we let the Church's theology of family and the human person guide our approach? We began by asking:

- What kind of family life does the Church's theology of family ask us to create?
- What attitudes about life and relationships does the Church ask faithful parents to convey?
- What can biology and the social sciences teach us about the best ways to achieve the goals the Church lays out for faithful families?

The original edition of *Parenting with Grace* was the fruit of this inquiry. In this all-new edition, we have broken *Parenting with Grace* into two volumes — one for parenting children from birth to age ten, and this book for parenting preteens and teens. We hope that this new structure will help parents apply the concepts that stand at the heart of Discipleship Parenting to each age and stage.

As with the first edition of *Parenting with Grace*, this book stands on insights drawn from Saint John Paul II's Theology of the Body. The Theology of the Body opened up new avenues of cooperation between theology and the sciences. In effect, the Theology of the Body teaches that *biology is theology*. That is, as we prayerfully reflect on God's design of the body — as revealed by science — we can learn a great deal about God's plan for life and relationships. Although many people focused on ways the Theology of the Body applied to marriage and sexuality, we argue that they apply just as much — if not, in some ways, more — to parenting. Since then, others have joined us in this assertion, including, most notably, Professor Mary Shivanandan of the Pontifical John Paul II Institute for Studies on Marriage and Family in her excellent book, *The Holy Family: Model Not Exception*. We are grateful for her endorsement of our work.

Although Saint John Paul's insights offered a fresh approach to integrating faith and science, his work stands on solid ground in the Catholic intellectual tradition. Saint Thomas Aquinas used to say that there are "two books" — the Bible (the book of God's Word) and the "Book of Nature" (i.e., science) — to which Catholics must turn to discover God's plan for anything. God is the author of all truth, discovered and revealed. He created the world (which science studies), and he gave us Scripture (which theology studies). Any authentic approach to studying either theology or science should confirm, not contradict, the findings revealed by either (cf. *Fides et Ratio*).

In the attempt to articulate a Catholic vision of anything — including parenting — the Church encourages us to be open to the insights that come from harmonizing both theology and science. Any approach that seeks to downplay one or the other is "less Catholic" than one that tries to integrate and harmonize insights from both.

This matters because there are lots of ideas about parenting out there, but not all of them pass muster when examined through this authentically Catholic lens. Some child-rearing advice is based on the assertion that "this is how I was raised, and I turned out fine" (whether or not that's really true). Other parenting ideas are based on scientific or quasi-scientific theories that can be difficult to reconcile with Catholic theology. Still other parenting approaches are based on a particular author's attempt to cherry-pick certain theological or biblical principles while ignoring science altogether. Many of the people promoting these ideas speak with authority and attract a wide following — even among Catholics. But that doesn't mean that their ideas actually represent an authentic Catholic view of anything, much less family life.

Of course, we all have to start somewhere. Everyone uses their own relationship with their parents, family, friends, as well as the resources with which they are most familiar as the starting point for their parenting careers. And yet the Catholic family isn't primarily a human institution. It's a divine one. United through the sacramental life of the Church, your common, ordinary, crazy family becomes something sacred, a "domestic church." By checking our basic assumptions about parenting against both the Church's vision and what science can teach about living out that vision in healthy ways, we can discover God's plan for parenting healthy, godly kids all the way through the preteen and teen years.

This is the approach we take in this book, just as we took in the first edition of *Parenting with Grace*. This book also includes findings from the Symposium on Catholic Family Life and Spirituality, which took place in the summer of 2019. For this truly historic event, our organization, the Pastoral Solutions Institute, worked in conjunction with the Our Sunday Visitor Institute, Holy Cross Family Ministries, and the Mc-Grath Institute for Church Life. We gathered almost fifty theologians, social scientists, pastoral counselors, and family ministry professionals, all of whom are internationally recognized for their work and research on faith and family life. Meeting for several days at the University of Notre Dame, the participants shared research from their respective disciplines, prayed together, and discussed the answers to four critical questions:

1. Are Catholic families called to be different from other fam-

ilies in the way we relate to one another in the home? If so, how?

2. What does an authentic, *family-based approach* to Catholic spirituality look like in practice?

3. What can the latest research tell us about creating a faithful home and raising faithful kids?

4. How can Catholic families be the outposts of evangelization and positive social change that Catholic teaching says they are meant to be?

The key insights developed in response to these questions are included in this edition of *Parenting with Grace*. That said, you don't have to take our word for it! If you're so inclined, we'd love for you to watch the various presentations at https://www.peytonfamilyinstitute.org or read *Renewing Catholic Family Life*, the book in which those presentations have been published. Regardless, by including the research from the symposium, we can confidently say that this latest edition of *Parenting with Grace* offers you the best, most current information both Catholic theology and the social sciences have to offer about raising healthy, happy, godly kids and building strong, grace-filled families.

On a personal note, when the first edition of *Parenting with Grace* came out in 2001, our oldest children, Jacob and Rachael, were still fairly young. Although we're still actively parenting, we're honored that our oldest children are now, themselves, practicing marriage and family therapists who have a profound love for Christ and deep heart for families. We're even more grateful that the Holy Spirit has called them to join us in promoting a uniquely Catholic vision of family life to a new generation. We're blessed by their contributions and insights.

What we most hope you'll take from this introduction is that whatever choices you make about raising your family — and whether or not you follow our advice in particular — as Catholic parents, we owe it to God and our kids to not just fly by the seat of our pants, casually parenting the way we were parented (good or bad), listening only to those sources that confirm our biases, or following any "expert" that doesn't make an honest effort to reconcile their assertions with *both* science *and* the Church's theology of family. Catholic parents certainly aren't obliged to all parent exactly the same way. But we are most definitely obliged to do all that we reasonably can to form our parenting consciences by opening our hearts to both the unique *Catholic* theology of family life (as opposed to secular or Protestant visions of the same) and what science can teach us about the healthiest ways to live out that vision.

We would also like to offer a word of encouragement to readers who may be unfamiliar with the approach to Catholic parenting outlined in the first volume of *Parenting with Grace* and who may be joining us in the middle of their parenting careers with somewhat older kids. Fear not! If you find anything that inspires you in these pages, feel free to jump in wherever you are and however you can. The success of the methods outlined in *Parenting Your Teens and Tweens with Grace* doesn't depend upon you having used them all along. Parents are often surprised at how quickly their kids respond to these methods and how dramatically their family lives benefit from this approach, even if they have been parenting in a completely different manner for years. Our goal is to help you build on the good things you have been doing all along and overcome any obstacles that might have been holding you back. We hope you will experience this book as a guide to help you be a more positive, effective, faithful parent, and that you feel free to use whatever you can however it makes the most sense in your particular circumstances.

The bottom line: God did write a parenting manual that will enable you to raise great kids, but to read it, you have to be willing to leave behind what's familiar and comfortable and go where the truths of both faith and science will lead you. Do not be afraid! With a little effort and openness to God's grace, you'll nail this parenting thing in no time.

Sincerely Yours in Christ,
Dr. Greg and Lisa Popcak
Jacob Popcak, MA, & Rachael Isaac, MSW

Holy Family, pray for us!

PART ONE

Being a Catholic Parent – What's the Difference?

But he said to me, "My grace is sufficient for you,
for power is made perfect in weakness." I will
rather boast most gladly of my weaknesses, in order
that the power of Christ may dwell with me.

2 Corinthians 12:9

Being a godly parent of preteens and teens is a wonderful job, but it's a tough one too! At its heart, being a Christian mom or dad means embracing the idea that "I don't have all the answers — *and that's okay."* The older our kids get, the more complicated parenting can become, and the more aware our kids are that we don't have all the answers. With other approaches to parenting, that can be intimidating, but with the approach we call "Discipleship Parenting," you don't have to be afraid that you don't know how to respond to all the challenges your kids present. In fact, it's better to admit to your preteens and teens when you don't automatically know what to do, instead of pretending and blustering like the Wizard of Oz in the hopes that your kids won't question your authority too much.

What preteens and teens respect more than anything is humility. They respect parents who are willing to say, "I'm not exactly sure how I feel about this/what to say about this/what to do about this, *but I know we can figure it out together!"*

Preteens and teens don't want parents who pretend they have all the answers. They want parents who can give them a thoughtful, reasonable, and graceful process for figuring things out for themselves. That process begins by admitting that you don't have all the answers and inviting your kids to join you in walking the steps of healthy Christian discernment. The earlier you start this process, the more your teens and young adults will internalize this process, freeing you from trying to control their every move, and shielding them from every negative influence so that you can be a guide, resource, and support to their growth into a healthy, godly adulthood.

The most important part of this process is knowing what you're aiming for. The Church teaches us that the entire point of parenting is not just raising kids who know the rules, but rather raising kids who are capable of intimate, caring, productive relationships with God, the people who will share their lives as adults, and communities in which they participate (see CCC 2214–2231). Helping your kids make good decisions today that will help them lead godly adult lives tomorrow starts with modeling the vision of family life to which the Church calls Christian households.

The next several chapters will explore six ways the Catholic theology of family calls Catholic parents to create a different sort of relationship — a discipleship relationship — with their children. By creating a discipleship relationship with your children, you are committing to working together with your kids to figure out how to live the Catholic vision of life and love in your daily lives as a family so that, ultimately, they can know how to live this vision in their own lives. For the purposes of our reflection, there are six ways God asks Catholic families to be different from other families. Practicing each of these ways will help you disciple your preteens and teens into a healthy adulthood.

They are:

1. God is our co-parent.
2. Our families are icons of the Trinity. The love we share in our homes isn't based on any human model — including our families of origin — but rather the self-giving, familial love we find at the heart of God.
3. Our families are domestic churches, and we are called to model ourselves after God's family, the Church.
4. We're on a mission to create communion, serve, live, bless others, and share Christ in all we do.
5. We turn to the saints for inspiration, guidance, and prayer support.
6. We recognize that parenting is a ministry that's meant to give the world what it needs most: the next generation of loving, godly people.

These six principles will be familiar to readers of *Parenting Your Kids with Grace (Birth to Age 10)*. While the principles in this volume are the same, this book has been developed to help you see their relevance to the preteen and teen years. We hope that rather than skipping ahead, you'll read through the chapters in this section with an eye toward how they can help you respond to the unique needs of your 11- to 18-year-olds.

CHAPTER 1

The First Difference: God Is Our Co-Parent

"By calling God 'Father,' the language of faith ... thus draws on the human experience of parents, who are in a way the first representatives of God for man."

CCC 239

Our children don't belong to us. They belong to God. God gives his children earthly parents because he wants them to be able to feel *his* love through your body and see his face in your eyes. Christian moms and dads are meant to be the face of God to our kids (see CCC 239)! This is particularly important to our preteens and teens. God made them to be their own persons, not little versions of us. Our teens need to know that the expectations we have for them, the rules we set, and the values we teach aren't just ways to manipulate them into being extensions of our own egos. They need to know that all of the lessons we're trying to teach them come from God and are ordered to help them become the people God wants them to be.

This is a big job. The good news is, you're not supposed to do it all by yourself. God wants to help you. But that might mean learning to pray a little differently than you're used to.

First, it is so important to pray *with your spouse every day*. Thank God for the gift of your family. Ask God to help you be the parents he created you to be. Ask him for the grace to be generous to each other and your children. Ask God to help you listen to what he is saying to you through the needs, concerns, complaints, and cares your teens bring to you, and ask him to help you respond as gently, thoughtfully, and generously as he would. If you haven't made a habit of praying daily as a couple, our book *Praying for (and with) Your Spouse* can help you painlessly learn the steps of creating a lifegiving couple prayer life.

Second, it's critical to pray with your kids every day, not just at formal prayer time, but all day long. If you're having a good moment, don't forget to pray. Out loud. With your kids. Don't be put off if it seems awkward, or if your kids roll their eyes or resist your efforts initially. That awkwardness or resistance doesn't mean praying together is somehow bad for you or that you're doing something wrong. It just means that you're doing something new. Prayer is an intimate activity. Taking any relationship to a deeper level almost always feels a little awkward at first. But the more you do this — even if you have to insist at first — the easier and more naturally it will come to all of you.

If you're not sure where to start, you might say something like, "Lord, thank you for letting me enjoy what amazing people my kids are becoming. Help me be the mom/dad you want me to be so I can keep helping them become everything you want them to be!" Similarly, if you're struggling, don't forget to pray. Out loud. With your kids. Say something like, "Lord, I'm kind of losing my mind right now, and my kids are pretty frustrated with me too. Help me be the parent they need me to be. Help me to listen — to you and to them — and be willing to work with them to figure out the best way to get through this together." Regardless of how awkward this might feel at first, the more you do it, the more God will bless you through it. Keep it simple. Keep it short. But pray from your heart and pray all day. Invite God to stand next to you all day as you parent. By all means, do whatever you can to carve out special time for prayer, reflection, and adoration, but don't reserve your faith for special times. Talk to God as if he were another family member standing right next to you and waiting to lend a hand. Because he is!

One tip we discuss in our book *Discovering God Together: The Catholic Parents' Guide to Raising Faithful Kids* is to teach your kids to pray over you. Hopefully, you have been giving your kids blessings by laying your hands on them and asking for God's grace for the day, or before special moments (like a test, game, or performance), or when they're hurting physically or emotionally. If you haven't been doing this, it's not too late to start, even if your children are now preteens or teens! Again, don't be put off by their eye rolls or resistance. It just means that your kids aren't used to relating to you on this level. A good practice is to get their buy-in before you spring this on them. During a family meeting or a one-on-one conversation, tell them that you would like to invite God to be more a part of your everyday life as a family. Talk about what that means to you and why you think it's important. Don't lecture and don't be abstract. Share from experience what your relationship with God means to you. Acknowledge that inviting God to be part of your lives this way might be a bit of an adjustment for everyone and normalize the fact that this might feel weird at first. Reassure everyone that it will get easier and more comfortable with practice. Then ask your kids to discuss any particular questions or concerns they might have. Just be sure to focus the conversation on making this kind of prayer easier or more comfortable for everyone. Don't imply that they won't have to do it if they raise enough objections or express enough concerns.

Once you've gotten their initial buy-in, make a habit of blessing your kids and asking God's blessing upon them. Once you've modeled this practice, you can also ask your teens to pray over you. We can't tell you how healing it is to be able to call your kids over and say, "I'm really having a tough day. Can you please pray over me?" and have your 14-year-old put his hand on your shoulder and say, "Lord, please give Mom your peace and help her be who you need her to be." Or have your 17-year-old pray, "Please help us know how we can support Dad as he goes through this. Let him know we love him and help us know how to be there for him." In the Popcak household, our children have been praying over us their whole lives — just as we have been praying over them all of theirs. Asking your teens to pray over you acquaints them with the spiritual power they've been given as sons and daughters of God. It also reminds them that when *we're* driving *them* crazy (hey, it happens …), they can go over our heads and talk to their heavenly Father, secure in the knowledge that he will help them out.

Of course, it's also good to create a little space every day for family prayer time. Dinnertime or bedtime are good times for many families, but you can do what works best for you. There are many different formats you can use for family prayer. One we developed uses the acronym **PRAISE**. This stands for:

> *Praise and thanksgiving* — Take turns acknowledging the blessings of the day.
> *Repentance* — Take turns asking God for the grace to handle the different challenges you faced today better the next time.
> *Ask for your needs* — Take turns asking for God's help with special intentions.
> *Intercede for others* — Take turns asking God to bless those who need our prayers.
> *Seek his will* — Bring all the decisions your family faces to God and ask for his wisdom to help you make the right choices so you can be the family he wants you to be.
> *Express your desire to keep listening* — As you wrap up, ask God for the grace to keep listening to his voice speaking to you through the events of the day so that you can continue to hear him until you meet together again in prayer.

Every family should feel free to tailor this format to their needs, integrating spontaneous or more formal prayers as you see fit. Our template allows you to create a meaningful family prayer ritual that "covers the bases" while still letting you tailor it to your family's needs. It can take as little as five minutes or as long as you like depending upon the time you have.

Another great resource for family prayer is the *Household Book of Blessings* published by the United States Conference of Catholic Bishops. It's a great book filled with family prayers and blessings for all occasions.

Of course, as Catholics we don't just enjoy the spiritual communion with Christ that prayer can facilitate. We experience Jesus "up close and personal" through the Eucharist. Human parents often say that their children are their "very own flesh and blood." Through Communion, we literally become God's very own flesh and blood. His Precious Body becomes one with our flesh, and his Precious Blood courses through our veins.

As the old church camp song says, there is "wonder-working power in the precious blood of the Lamb." Teach your children that as much as you love them, God loves them more. Teach that the Eucharist makes them God's sons and daughters even more than they're yours. We highly encourage regular Eucharistic adoration for families. The power of the sacraments shouldn't be underestimated. A friend of ours shared this story about how his relationship with Christ in the Eucharist helped him when his parents and teachers couldn't. Although he went to Catholic school, he was bullied mercilessly. By junior high, he was suicidal. Unfortunately, he kept this fact from his parents because he was ashamed, and he was pretty sure they couldn't help him anyway. Fortunately, God intervened in a powerful way:

> The one thing my parents always told me was that God loves me even more than they did and that even when I felt alone, I could always find God in the Eucharist. Eventually, out of desperation, I started sneaking into the church across the playground during lunch. At first, it was just to get away from the bullies, but in time I came to feel that God was calling me to him and holding me in his arms. I felt loved and protected in his presence. I would bring my concerns to him. I would pray for God to help me deal with the kids at school. He did that by giving me a real sense of how loved and precious I was in his eyes. Sometimes I even got in trouble for "hiding out" in church during recess. I guess the teachers thought I was up to something. I didn't care. God's love was the only thing that got me through those years. I wouldn't wish my experience on anyone, but I wouldn't give up that time I spent in God's presence for anything. The graces I received there helped me be the man I am today as much as anything my parents ever did — and they did a lot.

In sum, pray with your kids. Pray over your kids. Teach them to pray over you. Help them experience God's love in a personal way through all the sacraments. Teach them to think of God as the person who knows them best and loves them most. Just remember that all day, every day, God wants to parent alongside you and to fill in whatever gaps even your best efforts to love your kids will inevitably leave behind.

Prayer

Lord, help me to remember that my children are your children first and that you want to parent with me. Please come into every moment of my parenting life. Let me remember to lead my children in thanking you for the good times and asking you for help in the difficult times. Help me to experience your love more deeply in the Eucharist and to bring the love I find there home to my family. Help me lean more on the love, mercy, patience, joy, and strength that flows from your heart — especially when my own runs dry. Make me the parent you want me to be so that when my children look into my eyes, they will always see your loving face smiling back at them.

Holy Family, pray for us. Amen.

Questions for Discussion

What practical difference would it make if you were to behave as if God were parenting alongside you all day long?

What specific parenting challenges would you like to ask God's help with? How could you invite God into those moments when they are happening? What difference would it make for you to do so?

What ideas from this chapter would you like to start practicing today? How could you tailor these suggestions to your family?

CHAPTER 2

The Second Difference: Your Family Is an Icon of the Trinity

The primordial model of the family is to be sought in
God himself, in the Trinitarian mystery of his life.

Saint John Paul II, *Letter to Families*

The Christian family is a communion of persons,
a sign and image of the communion of the
Father and the Son in the Holy Spirit.

CCC 2205

The more we pray, especially when we pray in the honest, heartfelt manner we discussed in the last chapter, the more we reveal our inner life — our hopes, dreams, fears, and desires — to God. But because prayer is a conversation, the more we pray, the more God also reveals something about his inner life to us.

One of the things God has revealed to the Church about his inner life is that, in his very nature, *he is a family*. God is one God, but three

23

persons: Father, Son, and Holy Spirit. The love that exists between the three Persons of the Trinity is *familial.* As Saint John Paul put it, "God in his deepest mystery is not a solitude [i.e., an individual], but a family, since he has in himself fatherhood, sonship and the essence of the family, which is love."[1]

There's an important lesson in this for parents. We know God created us in his "image and likeness," but that doesn't only refer to us as individual persons. God also created the human family in his image and likeness, so that when people see the way Christian families love one another, they might get a little peek at what God's love looks like. That's why the Church calls Christian families "icons of the Trinity."[2]

The Challenge of Love

As you can imagine, there's a lot to unpack here. Entire books have been written on the subject, and we're not even going to attempt to scratch the surface about what all this theology means. But on a very practical level, one important takeaway for parents is that God calls Christian families to model themselves after him and the love that lives at his heart.

When parents argue about parenting, they usually do so because "your family showed love in one way and my family showed love in another way." As a Christian, the love you experienced in your family of origin is less important than the love God has in his heart for you and your kids. That's the love he wants us to learn to share with each other, little by little, day by day. God doesn't want us to show our family of origin's face to the world. He wants our families to show *his face* to the world. We must decrease so God may increase (see Jn 3:30).

This message is particularly important to teens. Preteens and teens are acutely aware of all the things that are wrong in the world, in their families, and in us. That can be intimidating. It can make us defensive. But if we are aware that our families are supposed to be icons of the love that is found at that heart of the Trinity, we can join them when they complain about things that aren't right at home. Instead of getting our backs up, we can say, "You know what? You're right. We do try our best to love you as God wants us to, but we're aware that there are lots of ways we fall short. How about this: Instead of sitting here arguing with each other about what our family isn't, let's start working together to figure out how to be more of the family God wants us to be. Where do you think we should start?"

This is a tremendously empowering exchange to have with your teens. It lets them know that, rather than Mom and Dad being the enemy, you are all on a journey together and, when one of you feels like you're off track, you can all work together to be part of the solution.

We all love our kids, but because we are sinful and broken, we are sometimes afraid to be as real and vulnerable with our teens as God wants us to be. That's a perfectly natural struggle. But by embracing the call to authenticity — to being real and vulnerable with one another — we unlock the power of the family to make us saints. Saints are simply people who have mastered the art of letting God see them for who they are and make them into who they're meant to be. Teens are all about figuring out who God is calling them to be. Our willingness to be vulnerable and embrace God's call to grow in our own lives gives them a model of growth our teens can respect and own for themselves. Teaching our teens how to acknowledge and embrace their need for godly growth is one of the best gifts we can give them, and the best way to give them this gift is to show them how we do it in our own lives.

The Big Question

If any of this seems overwhelming, remember Saint John Paul's admonition, "Be not afraid!" You're not alone. God wants to do this with you. The best way to start sharing the love that comes from the heart of the Trinity with your children is to prayerfully reflect on the following question every day:

> Given *both* the very real strengths *and* the very real limitations I'm dealing with, what's *one small thing I could do right now* to narrow the gap between the love/patience/compassion/generosity/mercy I'm naturally equipped to give my kids and the love/patience/compassion/generosity/mercy God wants to give my kids through me?

Don't try to do this on your own power. Pray for the grace to make this happen. Get the support of your spouse, your family, your faith community, a spiritual director, or even a professional therapist when necessary. But don't forget that Catholic parents are called to more than worldly parents are. No matter how great your family of origin was, it isn't enough to raise your teens the way you were raised. We're called to create families that are icons of the Trinity by allowing our hearts to be filled with God's love, and then generously sharing that love with our spouse and children. If there is anything standing in the way of our ability to do that, we're *obliged* as disciples of Christ to get whatever help we need to remove the obstacles so that our households can be the conduits of love that they are meant to be.

Prayer

Lord, let my family be a true icon of the Trinity: a home that radiates the love that comes from your heart inside and out. Help me to never settle for anything less than the love you want to give me and to never share anything less with my children than the love you want to give them through me. Give me the grace to use every moment of my parenting day as an opportunity to learn how to trade my human love for your godly love. Let me be patient with myself when I struggle or fail, but let me always keep this vision in mind so that even on my toughest, most imperfect days, I can remember to wrap them up in your arms and look at them through your eyes.

Holy Family, pray for us! Amen.

Questions for Discussion

What practical difference does it make to think of your family as an "icon of the Trinity"?

In what ways did your family of origin reflect the generous, abundant, merciful love that is found at the heart of the Trinity? In what ways did they struggle to do this? Practically speaking, how do you think God is calling you to give your children a different experience of adolescence than your parents were able to give to you?

Name one challenge you face in your relationship with your preteens or teens in which you'd like to do a better job of loving them with God's love or being more authentic with them. What would that look like in practice?

CHAPTER 3

The Third Difference: Your Family Is Part of God's Family

"The Father ... determined to call together in a holy Church those who should believe in Christ." This "family of God" is gradually formed and takes shape during the stages of human history, in keeping with the Father's plan.

CCC 759

"The Christian family constitutes a specific revelation and realization of ecclesial communion, and for this reason it can and should be called a domestic church." It is a community of faith, hope, and charity; it assumes singular importance in the Church.

CCC 2204

Most people have no idea how important family life is to God. So far, we've seen that God is like a family in his very nature, and that he created human families to live in his image. In this chapter, we'll look at how he created his own earthly family, the Church, to serve as a model for how Christian families are called to relate to one another.

The Catholic Church isn't just another= membership club. Catholics believe that the Church is, literally, God's family. Your domestic church, your household, is a branch of this divine family tree. The theme of family runs through every aspect of the sacramental life of the Church. For example:

- We're born into God's family through the baptismal font — which is literally considered the womb of the Church.
- The Eucharist is the family meal that God prepares for his children so that we might live forever.
- Confirmation initiates Christians into God's "family business": building the kingdom of God and bringing the world to Christ.

These are just a few examples.

From the beginning of time, God intended the human family to play a starring role in revealing his face to the world. Unfortunately, after the Fall, sin damaged the love and order God intended human families to live in. The world needed a model of the kind of family life God wants all of his children to experience. So, God sent his Son to establish the Church as his family on earth. By seeing how God "parents" his children through the Church, his children can learn to be godly families again.

The Catholic theology of family suggests that Catholic households should take our cues for how we relate to one another from the way God relates to us through his family, the Church. That's one of the deeper senses in which "the Church is a family of families."[1] As a "domestic church" your family is meant to be a "chip off the old block," so to speak. A little outpost of God's family in the world.

What can God's family, the Church, teach us about parenting teens? Lots! In this chapter, we'll explore five specific lessons we can learn by following the Church's example:

1. Connection is key
2. The sacred power of family meals

3. Self-donation is the key to obedience
4. Combine high standards with gentle discipline
5. Your home life is a liturgy

God's Family Tip #1: Connection is key

Preteens and teens spend a lot of time feeling alone, isolated, and unworthy. God understands this. He saw this sense of alienation emerge in his own children after the Fall. That's why he sent his Son to become one of us and gather us to him, so that we would never have to feel alone again. We could be his Church. His chosen people. His *family*. God makes us his family by *attaching himself* to us — and us to him — in a real and embodied way. He emptied himself and became one of us. He taught us. He healed us. He ate with us. He lived and worked and laughed and cried with us. Ultimately, he suffered, died, and rose for us. But Jesus Christ didn't just do all that way back when. The sacraments are God's family rituals that make Christ present to us today. Through these powerful, God-given rituals of connection, God continues to gather his family together, teaches us how to live in communion, forgives us when we fail, shows us how to do better, and gives us the love, nourishment, and support we need to become whole, healed, healthy, godly persons — just like he wants earthly families to do.

Following the example of God's family, the Church, Catholic parents are invited to make our domestic churches places that foster real *communion* by establishing and protecting strong family rituals. You might be surprised to know that teens especially need family rituals to give them a secure base from which to launch. Just as God's family is intentional about prioritizing the rituals that bring order to God's "house" (our parish church), Catholic parents should be intentional about creating strong family rituals that enable us to experience love, stability, peace, and joy in our households. Having regular rituals that enable your family to *work, play, talk, and pray* together at least a few minutes every day is critical to making your home a dynamic and soul-satisfying domestic church and giving your teens the sense of stability and structure they need to find their place in the world.

Rituals aren't just nice things families do once in a while. They are regular, intentional, planned (and, mostly, obligatory) times where families gather to work, play, talk, and pray together. Family rituals help teens know what it looks like to lead a healthy, holy, well-balanced life. When parents complain that their teens spend too much time on their phones, in front of video games, or obsessed with a boyfriend or girlfriend, the problem can often be traced to a lack of family rituals, which are meant to model what a balanced life looks like in the first place. By developing strong work, play, talk, and prayer rituals, families show their teens how a healthy, Christian person is meant to balance work, leisure, relationships, and faith.

- Examples of simple, daily *work rituals* include things like clearing the table together or cleaning up the kitchen as a family after meals, picking up the family room together before bed, folding laundry, or making beds together.
- Examples of simple, daily *play rituals* include things like taking a walk together, playing a board game or card game together, shooting hoops, working on a craft project or puzzle, or reading aloud.
- Examples of simple, daily *talk rituals* include discussing the highs and lows of the day over dinner or before bed, family meetings, and regular one-on-one time with a parent.
- Examples of simple, daily *prayer rituals* could include any of the things we discussed in the earlier chapters on praying together or any other type of prayer that helps you draw closer to God and one another.

Parents of teens often balk at this. Conventional wisdom says teens want *less* time with parents, not more. That's not entirely true. Research shows that healthy teens both want to spend time with their parents and have better social skills when they do.[2] Likewise, a large, international study found that teens who get at least six hours of family time per week get better grades, have greater social success, and are more mentally healthy than those who get less time with their families.[3]

Teens don't hate family time, but they do hate just sitting around the house, and they are terminally afraid of missing out. Because of this, if you don't have established rituals that enable you to *consistently* connect as a family, teens have a hard time understanding why all of a sudden Mom and Dad feel the need to do some random thing to create connection. It seems forced and, frankly, hypocritical to them. As we mentioned in our earlier discussion about introducing blessings and family prayer, it's helpful to not simply spring these changes on your kids, but also to try to get their buy-in first. Make some time in either a family meeting or in a one-on-one conversation to discuss what you want to do, why it is important to you personally, and how you think it will help you get to know them better. Elicit any concerns, questions, or suggestions with an eye toward making this more comfortable and doable for everyone, but don't imply that not doing this is an option. You aren't asking your kids' permission to strengthen family rituals. You are asking your kids' help to create rituals that are meaningful, workable, and lifegiving to your family relationships.

Despite any initial resistance, when a family cultivates regular rituals for working, playing, talking, and praying together, teens actually love it. They want a strong family life. They want to feel connected to Mom and Dad. But they need to be convinced of the commitment to keep up the relationship. They have little patience for one-off activities that allow Mom and Dad to check off the box and say, "On this date, I proved to myself that I was a good parent because I prayed/played a game/had a talk/did a project with my kid." Teens want either a real commitment from their parents, or they want their parents to get out of the way so they can have a relationship with the people who want to be committed to them. If your teens are sending you the message that they don't want to spend time with you, there is a good chance they aren't convinced of your commitment to creating an actual relationship with them.

Strong family rituals make your time together as a family more meaningful. Likewise, they clarify what constitutes family time and what constitutes "free time." If you don't have strong family rituals, you could spend all day together and still not feel connected. By contrast, if you make a commitment to do at least one thing every day to *work, play, talk, and pray together* as a family, it might take a total of forty-five to sixty minutes *combined*, but we guarantee it will change your life. It will make the time you spend together more meaningful and communicate clear expectations for when your teen needs to be home and when they are free to pursue their own interests.

Almost sixty years of research shows that the better established a family's rituals are, the more likely it is that they will be happy, stable, and close.[4] The same body of research shows that the more intentional a family is about creating rituals for working, talking, praying, and playing together, the easier it is for parents to pass on their faith and values to their kids — *without having to resort to lecturing and nagging.* We'll talk more about how you can create meaningful family rituals throughout this book. For now, it's enough to know that God's family, the Church, asks us to participate in so many rituals because they help us be happier, healthier people. They create a strong sense of identity and community, and they reinforce all the lessons God wants to teach his children about living a grace-filled life. They teach us how to relate, as Christian persons, to all the activities that make us fully human.

God's Family Tip #2: The sacred power of family meals

Speaking of meaningful rituals, the single most meaningful ritual God's family celebrates is the regular "family meal" we call the Eucharist. Through that meal, we learn that God is a hands-on parent. Any time we call on him, he takes time out of the busiest schedule in the universe to be there — body, blood, soul, and divinity.

Of course, the Eucharist isn't just some symbol. It's the actual Body and Blood of Christ. The Eucharist is the way God creates communion with his children. Inspired by the example of God's family, Catholic families are encouraged to celebrate meaningful family meals as a way of creating a sense of communion in the home. Pope Francis asserted the importance of meaningful family meals when he said, "A family that almost never eats together, or that never speaks at the table but looks at the television or the smartphone, is hardly a family."[5]

Mealtimes in the domestic church are meant to be a kind of sacred event. We don't mean they're sacred because they somehow involve holy water, perfect manners, good china, classical music, and locally sourced, organic produce. In fact, they're probably even more sacred when they're messy and noisy and simple. What makes family mealtimes a sacred event in your domestic church isn't all the trappings; it's that they are opportunities to share *yourselves* with each other, especially if you make a point of discussing topics that don't come up naturally. These can be things like the high and low points in the day, how you can better love and support one another, and what God might be trying to communicate to you (both individually and as a family) through the events of your day. By doing these things, you create real communion in your domestic church that feeds your family's soul.

Research by the University of Minnesota Eating As Teens (EAT) Project shows that teens who had regular family meals benefitted from stronger family relationships, had better social skills, and were at lower risk for delinquency and substance abuse.[6] Making a regular, meaningful family meal happen can be challenging, but it's an important way that Catholic families say to one another, "Other than God, you are the most important thing in the world to me. I promise to make the time to show you that every day at this meal."

God's Family Tip #3: Self-donation is the key to obedience

Through the sacraments we discover that God "commands" his children's obedience, not by bossing us around or scaring us into submission, but by giving us so much of himself that we can't help but want to draw closer to him. Even when sin makes us want to resist his love, he continues to give himself to us. Like a father who gently holds a fussy child until he melts — reluctantly but inevitably — into his loving embrace, God holds us in his arms until our tantrumming stops, our angry, pouting hearts melt, and we let him lead us.

"Self-giving" (also "self-donation") is a phrase that appears time and again in Saint John Paul II's writings. It means that just like God is immeasurably generous to us, he wants us to use everything he has given us — our time, treasure, talent, and even our bodies — to work for the good of the people he has placed in our life, starting with our spouse and children. Even though doing this sometimes feels hard, finding the courage to do it anyway is the key to becoming both happy and holy. As the Church says, we find ourselves by making a gift of ourselves.[7]

As you saw above, the Eucharist is a self-giving meal. It represents the most important way — out of a zillion other ways — that God gives all of himself to us and invites us to give all of ourselves back to him. Through this self-giving sacrament, God makes us want to offer our obedience freely to him as a loving response to the love he first gives us.

This is the model of discipline God wants human parents to use. Discipline rooted in a self-giving relationship with our teens makes true obedience possible. Instead of trying to command compliance using more and more desperate punishments, discipline rooted in a self-giving relationship enables us to capture our teens' hearts and form them in love. In his Theology of the Body, Saint John Paul made an important distinction between a moral ethos (where you do what is right out of love) versus a moral ethic (where you do what's right out of fear). This is an important distinction for parents. Would you rather your tween/teen behave out of a genuine love for you and desire to please you (moral ethos) or because they were simply afraid of getting caught doing something wrong (moral ethic)? In many ways, the source of our obedience matters even more than obedience itself.

Being appropriately but generously affectionate and affirming with our teens, gently correcting and guiding them, spending time doing projects and having fun with them, and making a real investment in developing our relationship with them can be very hard sometimes, but these simple practices become the way Catholic parents follow the self-giving approach to parenting that God models through the sacraments in his family, the Church. They are the ways parents lay the foundation for a moral ethos in our teens — a bone-deep desire to do what's right because it is the loving thing to do.

Both Saint John Paul's Theology of the Body and the science of neurology[8] teach us that human beings are literally wired to defer to those who make us feel cared for. It isn't just our mind that responds this way. Our body does too. For instance, scientists tell us hugs feel good because they allow the calmer person to, in a sense, "download" their emotional state into the more stressed-out person.[9] Hugs sync up the embracing couple's heart rate, respiration, and body temperature. The sigh you give when you get a really good hug means "Download complete. My body is now synced up with yours." That's what feeling connected to someone means. When we feel truly cared for, every part of us — our mind, body, and spirit — wants to "listen" and learn from the person who is giving themselves to us.

This is an important lesson for parents. You can try to force a tween/

teen to do your will (with decreasing success as they get older), but as soon as your back is turned, that young person will most likely look for ways to rebel against your authority. If you really want to command someone's heart — especially a teen's — being authentically self-giving is the only way to go.

This is exactly how God parents us. Parents follow the heavenly Father's example best when we take time to *listen* to our teens — not just with our ears, but with our whole selves — so that we can understand the needs and concerns on their hearts and help them address those needs and concerns in godly, fulfilling ways. The parent who does this commands their teen's obedience without having to threaten or bribe. Teens raised by genuinely self-giving parents learn the unconscious lesson that, "when I listen to my parents, they help me meet my needs in ways that not only make me happy, but also help me feel better about myself." Their obedience is easier to command because they want to willingly give it as a loving response to you having loved them first.

God's Family Tip #4: Combine high standards with gentle discipline

God's family, the Church, offers Catholic parents another parenting tip in the form of the Sacrament of Reconciliation. On the one hand, the members of God's family are held to tremendously high standards. God actually wants us to be saints! On the other hand, God is a tremendously gentle disciplinarian. Those "five Hail Mary" penances we get when we go to confession are not meant to punish us. They are meant to be opportunities to step into the role of the Prodigal Son (Lk 15:11–32), to be held in the Father's arms where we can experience a love so powerful that it makes us never want to leave home again.

Later in this book, we'll explore how you can have even higher standards for your tween's/teen's behavior employing loving-guidance methods rather than resorting to power struggles and attempts to impose heavy-handed punishments. For now, it's enough to know that if our heavenly Father can nudge us along the road to sainthood without losing his patience, maybe — just maybe — he can show us some tricks for getting our teens to pick up their socks without having to lose our minds.

God's Family Tip #5: Your home life is a liturgy
There is one final, critical lesson we can learn about parenting from God's family, the Church. Namely, the more we try to parent our children as God the Father parents us, the more our family life itself becomes a liturgy.

"Liturgy" is a word that refers to the way God "works" through his family, the Church, to heal the damage sin has done to our relationships with him and one another. The Liturgy of the Eucharist (i.e., Mass) restores our union with God and makes communion with others possible. In a complementary way, the Liturgy of Domestic Church Life enables you to bring Jesus home after you receive him so that he can continue to heal the damage sin has done to the relationships in your family and your world. Similar to the way that ordained priests preside over the Liturgy of the Eucharist, you could say that, through the common priesthood we received at baptism, Catholic parents preside over the Liturgy of Domestic Church Life. By seeking the grace to love one another with Christ's sacrificial love, Catholic mothers and fathers consecrate all the mundane aspects of family life and enable Christ to make them holy.

Do you know all those days where you feel like "what's the point?" Those days when you're worn out from being a bus service (or negotiating who gets the car), the laundry pile never seems to get any smaller, and all you want to do is run away and find something "important" to do? Realizing that your family isn't just a never-ending to-do list, but an actual living, breathing, domestic church that God wants to use to show you his love, make you holy, and help your kids be loved and holy too, stops you from living in survival mode. It reminds us that it's possible to thrive as parents — emotionally, relationally, and spiritually — because God's grace is hiding behind every broken heart, every social drama, every frustrating moment, and every tearful face. Instead of just white-knuckling your way through the next hassle that family life throws at you, remember that through it all, you are celebrating the Liturgy of Domestic Church Life. This will enable you to see that God is using every part of your parenting day — all those sleepless nights, frustrating experiences, and joyful moments — to help you do a better job of both receiving his love and sharing it with the children he has placed in your care.

All of the things you do to create a loving home aren't just "stuff you have to do." Driving your kids to the next activity, serving your family, helping your teens get their needs met in godly ways, and all the rest become the means by which God perfects you in grace as well as giving your kids a visible sign of how much God loves them. Celebrating the Liturgy of Domestic Church Life in your domestic church makes everything you do as a parent sacred and sacramental. When we do these things with God's love in mind, the Liturgy of Domestic Church Life heals the damage sin has done (and wants to do) to your family.

As a Catholic family you are truly blessed to live a different vision of family life than you can find anywhere else in the world. Your household isn't just a boring little place where boring little dramas are played out day in and day out. Your home is a divine institution, created by God to be an outpost of grace in the world. Your domestic church is a place where you and yours can be filled with the all-consuming, transforming love of God who cares about you so much that there isn't any single part of your life that he doesn't want to be involved in — especially the most boring and frustrating parts. And all you have to do is follow the Church's example to find grace hidden where you'd least expect it.

Prayer

Lord, help me to model my domestic church after your family, the Church. Help us to create strong rituals that bind us together in love. Help me to communicate my expectations for my children's behavior clearly but guide them gently. Let me "command" their obedience, not by the force of my will, but through the power of your love. And help me to celebrate the Liturgy of Domestic Church Life in a way that enables me to encounter your grace hiding just below the surface of everything we do to maintain our home and create a strong family life.

Holy Family, pray for us! Amen.

Questions for Discussion

What rituals did you have in your family as a teen? How did they bring you closer? What rituals for working, playing, talking, and praying together as a family do you have in your domestic church? How might you strengthen or build on them?

What does it mean for you to think of Christian obedience, not as a response to being forced or compelled to do something, but as a loving response to being loved? How might this idea challenge you to think differently about the way you "command" obedience from your tweens/teens?

What practical difference does it make to think about your family life as a Liturgy of Domestic Church Life that's intended to help you bring the grace of the Eucharist home and heal the damage sin has done to the relationships in your home?

CHAPTER 4

The Fourth Difference: We're on a Mission from God

The family finds in the plan of God the Creator and Redeemer not only its identity, what it is, but also its mission, what it can and should do. ... Hence the family has the mission to guard, reveal and communicate love, and this is a living reflection of and a real sharing in God's love for humanity and the love of Christ the Lord for the Church his bride.

Saint John Paul II, *Familiaris Consortio*, 17

As domestic churches, Catholic families are called to share in the "life and mission of the Church."[1] As far as the Church is concerned, every Catholic family is on a mission from God. When we do it intentionally and prayerfully, family life is a real, honest-to-goodness *ministry* that can transform hearts, make the world a better place to live, and call others to Christ. Although we usually think of "ministry" as "the churchy things we do at church," in reality "ministry" is any activity we engage in that conveys God's love to another person. If that doesn't describe Catholic family life, we don't know what does.

This is an especially important thing to remember for parents of tweens and teens because this age is all about discovering their gifts and learning how they can make a difference in the world. Teens need to be shown that making a difference in the world begins with living differently at home. True Christian service begins with responding to the needs of your closest neighbors — the people who live under your roof — promptly, generously, consistently, and cheerfully.

Saint John Paul II taught that your domestic church builds up the kingdom of God by committing to four critical tasks:

1. Create a deep, loving, and intimate communion in the home.
2. Serve life, both through our openness to having children and by diligently working to help the children we have be godly people at every age and stage.
3. Be a blessing to others both through the witness of our life as a family and through our service to our parish and community.
4. Share Christ with others, both through our faithful example as a family and through our mutual commitment to living the life and mission of the Church.

1. Create a deep, loving, intimate communion in the home.

Catholic parents respond to the Church's call to create deep, loving, and intimate communion in our homes both by making affection and connection job number one and by helping our kids experience the Faith as the source of the warmth in our home.[2] Research shows us that practices like generous, appropriate affection; loving-guidance approaches to discipline; and prompt, generous, and consistent responses to our tweens' and teens' needs are the best ways faithful parents can connect their children's hearts to the heart of God.[3]

The world says that work, school, and extracurricular activities come first and you fit family life in if you can. The Church asks us to treat family time as the most important appointment in our week and to commit to other activities only to the degree that they don't stop us from truly connecting with our spouse and children. As Pope Francis put it, one of the most important things parents can do to build the kingdom of God is to "'waste time' with your children."[4] Tweens and teens especially need time to hang out with Mom and Dad. Like toddlers, who take great joy in running away from Mom and Dad and even greater joy in running back to them, teens also need a secure base that keeps them anchored as they venture out into the world. Close family relationships in adolescence, rather than being stifling, give teens clear guidance on how much time they can appropriately spend with friends and provide teens a safe place to return to process the things they have experienced in the world. The closer the intimate communion you create at home, the more likely your teen will be to open up to you and seek your guidance about godly ways to respond to the challenges they encounter in their school and social lives.

2. Serve life, both through our openness to having children and by diligently working to help the children we have be godly people at every age and stage.

Catholic parents' commitment to serve life essentially involves two things. First, that even as your children are getting older, you and your spouse ask God every day to make you open to the children he wants to give you — whether that means that your family may ultimately be either bigger or smaller than you, yourself, envisioned. Second, that you and your spouse ask God every day to help you give your children everything they need to grow up to be healthy, godly men and women who can glorify him with their lives. Balancing these two goals stands at the heart of what the Church calls "responsible parenthood" — that is, cultivating an openness to life that is respectful of the need to raise fully formed, godly persons. Each day, we should sit down with our spouse and offer a prayer that goes something like this:

> Lord, we give our hearts and our family to you. Help us to be open to having the children you want to give us. And help us raise the children we have in your love, so that they may come to know you and never depart from you. Make us the family you want us to be.

Remember, our family belongs to God. If we truly want to be a godly family, we have to regularly ask him want he wants for us. Of course we have a say in how it all works out. In fact, we have quite a lot of say. God, in his mercy, is deeply respectful of our needs, concerns, strengths, and limitations. Moreover, he wants us to be respectful of *our* needs, concerns, strengths, and limitations — because we will struggle to raise godly kids if we aren't (see chapter 9). Children are certainly a great blessing from the Lord (Ps 127:4–5), but the most important thing for Catholics is not the number of children we have. Rather, it is doing our best to provide all the children God gives us with everything they need to be godly adults. "For one can be better than a thousand; rather die childless than have impious children!" (Sir 16:3).

Ultimately, God knows us best and loves us most. The call to serve life is a call to prayerfully discern God's vision for both our family size and family dynamic. In this way, we can discover how to build a domestic church that glorifies God and fully respects our unique strengths and struggles.

3. Be a blessing to others, both through the witness of our life as a family and through our service to our parish and community.

We live in a hurting world. As domestic churches, we don't just live for ourselves. We're called to share God's love with the world in whatever ways make sense based upon our family's current state in life. As parents of tweens and teens, your kids will be looking to you to discover healthy ways to make a positive difference in the world.

As a Christian home, don't fall into the trap of relegating charitable service to special service projects. Make serving one another and the world part of your everyday family life. Regularly work as a family to gather gently used clothes, toys, and other items and take them, together, to your local mission. Work together to make meals for sick, pregnant, or elderly neighbors. Practice the ministry of hospitality by making your home a place for godly fun and fellowship. These are just a few examples of ways you can think of others while being a family at home. The website DoingGoodTogether.org offers many suggestions for family service in the home and in the community.

That said, a word of caution is in order. We've encountered many well-meaning, faithful parents who thought that if they just dedicated their lives to serving others — even if it meant sacrificing strong family rituals and an intimate home life — their teens would learn the importance of Christian service. More often what happens is that kids become resentful. While serving others is important, when parents only seem to care for people with problems, our teens can begin to think they must become people with problems in order to get us to care about them. Although it is a common notion that teens are drawn to trouble because they think it makes them "cool," this idea does not represent the full picture. Antisocial behavior tends to convey the implicit message that "I am strong, powerful, above the rules, and able to get things done." This message can make people seem, superficially, more socially desirable. In other words, teens are not naturally drawn to trouble. They are drawn to the social status and social connections that trouble can foster. The more parents give teens a healthy, positive way to make connections and feel connected, the less attractive unhealthy ways to make connections become. Strong family rituals make this kind of healthy connection possible.

The good news is that there are about a bazillion-and-one ways your family can work *together* to be a blessing to others and simultaneously develop a stronger relationship with your kids. We'll explore more ways to do this throughout the book.

4. Share Christ with others, both through our faithful example as a family and through our mutual commitment to living the life and mission of the Church.

You probably know any number of people — friends, extended family members, coworkers — who would most likely never darken the door of a church. How are you sharing Jesus with them? Teens, in particular, are wired to seek causes to serve. How are you helping your tweens and teens discover ways they can respond to the most important cause of all: sharing Christ with others?

Don't let this question intimidate you. Sharing Christ with others doesn't have to be an onerous or even deeply religious task. For instance, at the Symposium for Catholic Family Life and Spirituality, Pat Fagan, the director of the Marriage and Religion Research Institute (Marri.us), expressed the wish that every Catholic family would host an annual barbecue/block party for their neighbors. They wouldn't have to do anything except be hospitable, give everyone a chance to get to know one another better, and provide some wholesome games or entertainment. The only religious thing they would need to do was offer a thoughtful, heartfelt prayer of blessing before the meal. Your tweens and teens could play an important role in organizing these events, helping you cook, planning/supervising games for the smaller children in attendance, etc. The event would be a whole-family affair!

He imagined that the host family wouldn't see any fruit right away, maybe not even for years. But one day, out of the blue, the husband or wife — or even one of the older teens — would hear from a neighbor who would say, "Listen, you're, like, a Christian, right? Can I ask you something?" It might be a question about their marriage, or their kids, or some faith topic, or anything at all. But now the door is open, and the Catholic family barely had to do anything. At the very least, the Catholic family on the block would establish themselves as caring people who want to bring others together. That's two-thirds of what good evangelization involves.

Think of how the world would change if every Catholic family on the planet did just this much. And that's only one idea. In *Discovering God Together: The Catholic Guide to Raising Faithful Kids*, we offer a ton of great tips for how your family can bring Christ to the world through your example of love.

Your Family Mission and Charism

A big part of the job description for an adolescent is discovering their mission and charism. Don't leave the job of helping your teens develop their mission and charism to their teachers, coaches, youth ministers, or peers! You can help your teens get a leg up on this developmental challenge by making sure that you have developed your family's mission and charism. A family mission helps you identify the qualities God wants your family to practice to live a more abundant life together. A family charism clarifies the ways your family can use the gifts and talents God gave you to be a blessing to others. Having a clear family mission and charism helps teens intuit the process of discerning their own. It also establishes Mom and Dad's credibility in their teens' eyes as the go-to people for helping them discern this for themselves. Here are some simple tips you can use to begin developing your family mission and charism.

Family Mission

God didn't bring you together by accident! He created your family so that you could build the kingdom in a special way that's unique to you. Although each person in your family is different, you share a life in common. Because of that, there are probably some virtues (like respect, joy, love, justice, mercy, generosity, peace, compassion, etc.) that would be of special importance in your house. Likewise, as a family, you may have certain interests, talents, or skills (e.g., music, sports, arts and crafts, teaching, service, hospitality, organization, etc.) that you have in common.

To determine your family mission, pray as a family over time about the qualities or virtues that you think are most important to living a good, godly life together. As you think about the different personalities in your home, what are the virtues you need to practice most to create a loving, joyful, faithful, orderly family? Below are examples of some virtues that could be the basis of your family mission. Feel free to come up with others that fit your family life more accurately. Choose three to four qualities/virtues that will be the foundation of your family mission.

Love	Generosity	Compassion
Service	Respect	Peace
Joy	Kindness	Self-Control
Patience	Faith	Wisdom
Prudence	Doing Right	Life Balance

List others here: _____

_____

Now organize these qualities in the form of a family mission statement.

We are the (Name) family. We have been called together by God to live lives of (insert qualities here) in our relationships with one another and everyone we meet.

Review this mission statement regularly over family meals or in family meetings. Reflect on what you are doing to live out these qualities in the way you relate to one another, your decisions as a family, and your interactions with others. Ask one another what you could do to be better examples of these qualities in your personal lives and in your life as a family. Consider these qualities in the decisions you make. What choices would help you do a better job of living out these virtues? What choices would make it more difficult?

Over time, continue to pray about your family mission. Is God asking you to practice different virtues as your circumstances change? Let your family mission statement draw you together to strengthen your family and build the kingdom of God in your own unique way. Later, in the chapters on developmental tasks, we'll return to the topic of helping your teens develop their own missions. For now, teach them to think in these terms by raising them in a household rooted in a strong family mission.

Family Charism

To discern your family charism, prayerfully reflect on gifts, talents, or interests you share in your family. Examples include things like sports, music, art, performing, hospitality, service, hard work, building, creating, teaching, leading, helping, etc. List these below.

God has blessed our family with the following gifts, talents, and interests:

_____

_____

_____

Now, as a family, prayerfully reflect on the question, *How can we bless others with the gifts, talents, or interests we share?* You might have certain gifts, talents, or interests in common, or you might see creative ways to combine the different individual gifts, talents, or interests you have. The answer to this question provides insights into the charisms you have been given. A charism is more than a gift, talent, or interest. It is a gift, talent, or interest that is consecrated to God and used to bless the Body of Christ.

Just as God calls different religious orders (Franciscans, Jesuits, Benedictines, Salesians, etc.) to bless the world with their unique missions and charisms, every domestic church is called together by God to serve his kingdom in some unique way. Your family has every bit as important a part to play in building the kingdom of God as any official religious order. As the *Catechism* puts it, "The Christian family constitutes a specific revelation and realization of ecclesial communion" (2204). Whether you realize it or not, your Catholic household is meant to be a *bona fide* ministry and outreach of the Church. Discerning your family mission and charism enables you to deepen your understanding of all the ways God wants to use your household to be a blessing to the world.

Again, we'll return to the topic of helping your kids develop their own charism later in the book. That process will be a lot easier, and make a lot more sense, if you raise your children in a family that regularly discusses your charisms and the ways God is using your family to bless others.

Conclusion

Don't ever feel that you aren't doing great things for the kingdom because you're busy with the business involved in running your family. All of these simple activities are part of the Liturgy of Domestic Church Life that, done lovingly and prayerfully, enable you to be outposts of God's love in the world. By doing the best you can to live out the four critical tasks and discern your family mission and charism, your family becomes a true ministry, equipped by God's grace to communicate his love to the world and participate in his plan to heal the damage sin has done to all of our relationships.

Prayer

Lord, help my family, my domestic church, be mindful of our mission to create an intimate communion in our home, to raise each child you give us to love you with all their hearts, to be a blessing to those in need, and to bring Christ to everyone we know. Make us your outposts of love and grace in the world so that, through our witness, we can draw the whole world to you.

Holy Family, pray for us! Amen.

Questions for Discussion

How did your family of origin live out the fourfold mission of a Catholic family (Create Communion, Serve Life, Be a Blessing, Share Christ)? Would you want your parents' example to impact the way you and your children live out this fourfold mission? If so, how?

In what ways does your domestic church already live out the fourfold mission of Catholic families (whether intentionally or not)? What is one thing you could do to live each of the four missions more intentionally?

How do you think identifying your family mission or charism would help you experience God's grace more fully or serve others more effectively?

CHAPTER 5

The Fifth Difference: We Aren't Too Proud to Listen to Our Older Brothers and Sisters

"Being more closely united to Christ, those who dwell in heaven fix the whole Church more firmly in holiness. ... They do not cease to intercede with the Father for us, as they proffer the merits which they acquired on earth through the one mediator between God and men, Christ Jesus. ... So by their fraternal concern is our weakness greatly helped."

CCC 956

Catholic parents are never alone. The saints always have our backs. We just have to call on them!

We should start by always seeking the Holy Family's help. In our home, we ask for the Blessed Mother's intercession for everything from seeing that we don't burn dinner, to helping us correct our children as gently as she corrected Jesus when he was getting underfoot (being sinless doesn't mean he was never in the way!). Likewise, we regularly ask

Saint Joseph to coach us in being patient, loving, generous, faithful, and strong parents who put God's will before our own. The love the Holy Family shared and the example they set isn't just some abstract ideal; it's a model for all families.[1] The more we reflect on them and ask them for their prayers, the more we can become like them.

A Special Saint for Parents

Saint John Bosco is another really important saint for Catholic families. He wasn't a parent, but he was a great Christian teacher and the founder of a religious order (the Salesians) dedicated to helping and educating children. Many of the students Saint John Bosco taught were homeless or delinquent. At the time, people believed that children in general — and these kids in particular — were little better than animals who responded only to physical punishment and harsh correction. One day, the Blessed Mother visited Saint John Bosco in a vision. She told him that children should be corrected, "not with blows, but with sweetness and charity."

Deeply moved by this vision, Saint John developed a system of discipline he called the preventive system, in contrast to what he considered to be the heavy-handed repressive system of his day. He taught his followers that even the most willful, defiant children would offer their heartfelt obedience if they were treated with love and respect. He argued that Christian discipline shouldn't just be about getting kids to behave. It had to be about evangelizing children in the way of love and virtue. He said that his method "consists in making known the rules and regulations ... and then supervising in such a way that the students are always under the vigilant eye of the [caregivers], who like loving fathers will converse with them, act as guides in every event, counsel them and lovingly correct them, which is as much as to say, will put the [children] into a situation where they cannot do wrong."

Saint John Bosco never wanted to lead his students into temptation. He preferred to focus on teaching children what to do and then supporting their success as opposed to ignoring children until they misbehaved and then punishing them after the fact. The preventive system forms children's characters through "reason, religion, and loving-kindness." Regarding the harsh punishments popular in the day, the saint famously said, "To strike [a child] in any way ... should be absolutely avoided, because ... they greatly irritate the young, and they degrade the educator." In this, he echoed the sentiments of another great saint, Saint John Chrysostom, a Doctor of the Church (an official Church title given to saints whose teachings are especially important to understanding our faith) who said, "Accustom (your child) not to be trained by the rod; for if he feel it ... he will learn to despise it. And when he has learnt to despise it, he has reduced thy system to naught."

We're unaware of any other saint besides John Bosco who has offered the Church such a comprehensive system of child rearing, but other holy men and women, such as the Boys and Girls Town founder, Servant of God Father Ed Flanagan, and famed Catholic educators Maria Montessori and Sophia Cavalletti (who developed the Catechesis of the Good Shepherd, an approach to religious education based on Montessori's methods), also advocated similar loving-guidance approaches to discipline. All of these great Catholic men and women recognized that the best way to help children be their best was to uphold remarkably high standards but support their success via the gentlest means. We'll discuss many gentle, remarkably effective discipline techniques in future chapters. But for now, it's enough to understand our basis for asserting that a loving-guidance approach to discipline is more consistent with our Catholic Faith.

In addition to turning to the saints for inspiration in your family life, don't forget to introduce your tweens and teens to the saints that can inspire them. Look up stories of their patron saints (i.e., the saint for whom they are named or their confirmation saint). Read brief stories of the lives of the saints and encourage your teens to take initiative in learning more on their own as well. Lead your tweens and teens in asking the saints who are important to them and your family for guidance and looking to their lives for inspiration.

Just as you might message your best friend for sympathy or support, and your teens are likely to do the same, don't forget to ask for the saints' intercession as well — especially on those tough days when you feel like you don't have an ounce of strength left or a friend in the world. Asking for the saints' help is more than a pious practice. It's a lifesaver!

Prayer

Lord Jesus Christ, help me to correct your children like your Mother instructed Saint John Bosco to correct the children you placed in his care: "with sweetness and charity." Help me to remember how patient and merciful you are with me when I fail you. Give me the grace to extend similar mercy to my children when they let me down and frustrate me. Let me always choose methods of correction that are rooted not in fear, but love, and help me model the way of love and virtue in my relationship with them. Let me show my children that following your way is not just the right thing to do, but the path to a happy, healthy, holy life.

Holy Family and Saint John Bosco, pray for us! Amen.

Discussion Questions

How do you ask for the saints' intercession to help you be a godly, effective parent?

How do Saint John Bosco's teachings challenge or support your ideas about good, faithful discipline?

In what situations do you most need God's grace to correct more gently or charitably? What would you do differently? What saint will you ask for help to follow through with this resolution?

CHAPTER 6

The Sixth Difference: Parenting Is a Ministry

So great and splendid is the educational ministry of Christian parents that Saint Thomas has no hesitation in comparing it with the ministry of priests: "Some only propagate and guard spiritual life by a spiritual ministry: this is the role of the sacrament of Orders; others do this for both corporal and spiritual life, and this is brought about by the sacrament of marriage, by which a man and a woman join in order to beget offspring and bring them up to worship God."

Saint John Paul II, *Familiaris Consortio*, 38

By now you know that family life is neither an obstacle to living a holy life nor to doing important work for God's kingdom. But as we bring part one to a close, we wanted to emphasize that *Catholic parenting and family life are truly ministries* in the eyes of the Church.

How you parent really matters, not just to your kids, but to your Church, your community, and yes, to God. Your work as a Catholic parent is an actual ministry. As we mentioned in chapter 4, "ministry" isn't just the "churchy stuff we do at church." It is any activity that communicates God's love to another person. As we prepare our teens to find the missions, charisms, and causes they will serve, it is critical that we show them that working to have strong, healthy, godly relationships is the most important ministry to which they can commit their time and energy.

The Church teaches that family life is the most important ministry work moms and dads can do! That's another sense of the phrase "domestic church." Being a lector, or leading the music at Mass, or even volunteering for a charity are all wonderful ministries, but God would have an easier time finding someone else to do any of those things than he would finding someone else to lead your children to him. Catholic parents are meant to build the kingdom of God primarily by dedicating themselves 100 percent to creating joyful, loving, godly homes and raising joyful, loving, godly kids. By modeling prompt, generous, consistent, and cheerful service in the home and teaching our kids to participate in this spirit of service, we prepare them to think of charity not as something we do once in a while for "those poor unfortunate people over there," but as a way of responding to any person we encounter — especially the people we are closest to. Think of how different the world would be if every Catholic family took this mission seriously.

Many Catholic parents feel selfish thinking of parenting as ministry. They often tell us it feels like trying to get credit for something they'd have to do anyway. Frankly, this view reveals the unintentional "do whatever works for you" approach most people have toward parenting. What makes parenting a ministry isn't the fact that you do it; it is the way you do it. No, parenting isn't a ministry if you roll out of bed and mindlessly trudge through the day, day after day. But if you do your best — in the face of your very real limitations and struggles — to fill every interaction with your kids with Christ's love, you will change the world.

There is an entire science called *ethnopediatrics* that studies the effect parenting styles have on the culture at large. We tend to think that culture is mainly about language, the arts, religion, etc. But long before people engage in any of these cultural activities, they are parented.

In her book, *Our Babies, Ourselves,* Cornell anthropologist Meredith Small argues that a culture's approach to parenting shapes that society's use of language, its approach to the arts, the values and worldview it promotes, and even its attitude toward spirituality, faith, and values.

As Saint John Paul famously said, "As the family goes, so goes the nation and so goes the whole world in which we live." Small argues that the parenting methods advocated by a particular culture do more to impact its worldview than almost any other factor.

Of course, there's no guarantee that a particular parenting style will automatically produce children who are perfect models of a culture's values. But, Small argues, different cultures advocate different parenting practices because they've found, through centuries of trial and error, that certain parenting practices are consistently significantly more likely to promote certain values than other parenting practices.

Why is this important to Catholic parents? Because Catholics are called to evangelize the culture.[1] The Church challenges Christian families to build a "civilization of love" filling the world with children who are capable of exemplifying the self-giving love that comes from the very heart of God.

Most of us aren't going to create great works of art, develop new languages, or come up with brilliant theological or philosophical insights, or even perform heroic acts that will be spoken of for generations. But every single Catholic family can choose to parent in a way that shows what God's generous, joyful love looks like in practice. The world desperately needs godly, loving, generous people. As Catholic parents, you are in the best position to give the world exactly what it needs. The way you parent your children today will affect the world for generations to come. The example you set will become the example your children and grandchildren will most likely default to in parenting their own children.

As we already mentioned, "self-giving" is the virtue that most clearly defines the civilization of love that Catholic parents are called to build. When Catholic parents follow Christ's example of self-giving love in our relationship with our kids, we not only grow in personal holiness, but we also celebrate the power of the ministry of family life to transform the world through our example.

If you would like to learn more about how to relate to parenting as a ministry, check out our books *Discovering God Together: The Catholic Guide to Raising Faithful Kids* and *The Corporal Works of Mommy (and Daddy Too!)*. We would also like to invite you to sign up for The Catholic HŌM, a parenting program available for parishes or online at CatholicHom.org. Likewise, we hope you'll take advantage of the online courses we developed for the Ministry of Parenting track through the Catechetical Institute at Franciscan University at https://www.catechetics.com.

Prayer

Lord, help me to always remember that parenting is my primary ministry; that the way I parent is the most important way you show your children how much you love them. Help me build a strong domestic church. Show me how to make our family a light to the world that draws others to you — not just in spite of our weaknesses, struggles, and challenges, but in the way we respond to our weaknesses, struggles, and challenges. Make us a family after your own heart.

Holy Family, pray for us. Amen.

Questions for Discussion

What does it mean to you to think of parenting as a ministry? How does it change the way you view your role — especially as a parent of tweens/teens?

What messages does your relationship with your tweens/teens communicate about the way God loves them? What might you want to change in your relationship with your kids so that you could more effectively communicate God's love to them?

What message do you think your family life sends to others about the ability of your Catholic faith to create warm, loving, joyful, generous people? What message does your family life send to your teens about the role of the family in building the kingdom of God?

What small changes might you want to make to become an even better witness to the power of God's love in your home? What support might you need to make those changes?

• • •

Conclusion to Part One

So, there you have it! Catholic families are called to be different from other families in the way they relate to one another and the world because ...

- God is our co-parent, and we prayerfully invite him into every part of our day.
- Our families are icons of the Trinity. The love we share in our homes isn't based on any human model — including our families of origin — but rather the self-giving, familial love we find at the heart of God.
- Our families are domestic churches that model ourselves after God's family, the Church.
- We're on a mission to create communion, serve life, bless others, and share Christ in all we do.
- We turn to the saints for inspiration, guidance, and prayer support.
- We recognize that parenting is a ministry that's meant to give the world what it needs most: the next generation of loving, godly people.

The Church will never say, "Here are the parenting techniques you must use to be a great Catholic parent," but as you see, she does present very clear ideas about how Catholic families are called to live and the mission Catholic parents are called to serve. Likewise, science offers important insights about the kinds of parenting practices that can help Catholic parents live out this vision in practical, meaningful, and manageable ways. The most "Catholic" method of parenting is the one that draws its recommendations from Saint Thomas Aquinas' "two books" of revelation: faith and science.

Adolescence is a time when kids become much more sensitive to the need to find their mission and calling. Raising them in a Catholic household where the idea of mission is woven into the daily life of the family is the best way to help your teens understand what living life as Christian disciples really looks like. Having a mission is ultimately about intentionally living for God and claiming the world for Christ. Neither of those things begins when you leave your house. They start when you open your eyes in the morning. Your mission serves as the basis of all of your relationships. It informs even the most mundane tasks of your everyday life. There is nothing you do all day that God doesn't want you to do for him. There is no person you encounter throughout your day — at home or away — that God doesn't want you to bring his love to through your words or actions. Living your life — not just as some worldly family, but as a true "domestic church" — enables you to show your children how to live as godly men and women for others in everything they do, from the moment they get up in the morning to the moment they close their eyes at night. Your ability to live your family mission — by intentionally discerning and discussing how your family can live for Christ and call the world to Christ — is, in large part, what determines whether your teens will come to see "faith" and "values" as things that are integral to their daily life, or whether they are just optional traits to trot out on Sundays or when religious conversations come up.

Having explored the general vision of living the Catholic difference at home, let's look more closely at what all this looks like in practice and give you the tools you need to build your dynamic domestic church and raise your preteens and teens to be loving, godly disciples of Christ.

PART TWO
Discipleship Parenting

Catholic parents aren't just called to raise kids. We're called to raise passionate followers of Jesus Christ — young men and women who know how to love God with all their hearts, minds, souls, and strength and their neighbors as themselves (see Mt 22:37–39). More than parenting teens, Catholic parents are called to *disciple* them into a healthy, godly adulthood.

Over the years, we have searched for an appropriate name for the kind of parenting style we advocate. Recently, a friend and colleague of ours, author Kim Cameron-Smith, coined the term "Discipleship Parenting." We're happy to recommend her excellent book, *Discipleship Parenting: Planting the Seeds of Faith.* With her gracious permission, we also use this term to describe our approach.

Discipleship Parenting is the process by which the child's heart is turned (and re-turned) toward his parents at every stage of development so that Mom and Dad can ultimately bring their child's heart to God. Through this process, parents also learn to hear God's voice speaking to them through their teens, inviting them to grow and heal as well. Discipleship is a relationship where both the follower and the mentor help *each other* grow closer to God through the process of accompaniment.

In the following chapters, you'll discover what science can teach us about the most effective ways to train your teens in the way they should go, so that even as adults they will not depart from it (see Prv 22:6).

CHAPTER 7

Having a Ball: Discipleship and Attachment

Go, therefore, and make disciples.

Matthew 28:19

*Let the children come to me ... for the kingdom
of heaven belongs to such as these.*

Matthew 19:14

Being a Discipleship Parent begins with cultivating healthy attachment with your child. Now, chances are, if you have heard people use the term "attachment" with regard to parenting, you may have been led to believe that it applies solely to practices used with infants and toddlers (e.g., extended nursing, co-sleeping, baby wearing, etc.). It does not.

Fostering healthy attachment *at any stage* of your child's development (from infancy through adulthood) means responding to your child's needs promptly, generously, consistently, and cheerfully and, as they get older, helping your child learn to respond to others' needs in a similar way. Although your child's developmental needs will change from year to year, your ability to develop strong attachment with your child is dependent upon your ability to (1) respond promptly, generously, consistently, and cheerfully to those needs, whatever they are; *and* (2) help your child learn how to give back to whatever degree they are able.

What are commonly understood to be attachment parenting practices in infancy do help parents respond well to the needs of infants and toddlers, but they don't do anything to help parents respond to the needs of kids in early childhood, middle childhood, pre-adolescence, or adolescence. Discipleship Parents must either continue to build or, in some cases, rebuild attachment at each stage. We do this by learning how to be the primary person our child turns to for help in meeting their developmental needs in godly and fulfilling ways.

Although this book's focus is the tween and teen years, it can be helpful to see how attachment develops as a continuum. To that end, this chapter will first give you a brief glimpse at what secure attachment looks like at every stage. Then, we'll help you understand how your ability to disciple your child is directly related to secure attachment. Finally we'll help you see how it's never too late to build stronger attachment with your kids, even if you're just starting out in the tween and teen years. We'll offer additional tips for building strong attachment with older kids in the chapters that focus on developmental issues.

Play Ball!

At any stage, building strong attachment with your kids is a lot like playing catch. When you play catch, you watch how the other person throws the ball, and you try to throw it back in ways that they can catch it. Sometimes, you might mix things up. Maybe you throw it faster or slower. Maybe you throw a curveball once in a while. It can be fun to mix it up, but the goal isn't to intentionally make the other person miss. In a good game of catch, you try to help each other get better at sending the ball back and forth in a variety of ways, and you try to keep the ball in play no matter how it's thrown to you.

In a similar way, Discipleship Parents work to maintain strong, supportive back-and-forth interactions with their teens so they can maintain good communication and rapport (both verbally and nonverbally). In this way, the *relationship itself* becomes the primary way Discipleship Parents share the Faith with their teens and lead them closer to God.

Discipling anyone in the Faith — especially adolescents — isn't as much about "telling" them as it is about *relating* to them (or as Pope Francis puts it, "accompanying").

Through the back-and-forth process of consistent, supportive responding and relating, the teen communicates his or her needs to the parent, and the parent responds promptly, generously, and consistently to the teen. Through this process, teens learn how to identify and meet their needs in healthy, godly ways.

Over time, by playing this relational "game of catch" around all the issues that develop the adolescent's character, faith, and morals, your teen learns that there is nothing they can throw at Mom or Dad that they can't handle. Parents might drop the ball once in a while, but never on purpose, and they always pick it back up again. Parents who cultivate this kind of relationship with their teens are much more likely to raise young adults who are happy to have caught all the lessons their mom and dad have thrown to them over the years.[1]

Yerrrr OUT!

But let's change up the game. Imagine playing catch with someone who was so distracted that they only threw the ball back every tenth time. Or what if every time they missed the ball, they made you chase it and blamed you for throwing the ball incorrectly? Or what if every time they threw the ball, they intentionally tried to *make* you miss it, and then criticized you for not having your head in the game? Even if these terrible teammates regularly took you to baseball games and read you books about great baseball players, would you know how to play the game? Would you want to? More likely, you'd be relieved when you finally got to leave the team and give it all up so you wouldn't have to feel so frustrated all the time.

All of these latter examples are ways that parents undermine their ability to disciple their teens. The more we fail to respond to our teenagers' needs, blame our kids for the breakdowns in our relationships with them, criticize and lecture them instead of actively helping them succeed, or use heavy-handed punitive parenting techniques that shame our kids instead of helping them learn from their mistakes, the more our teens eventually get tired of playing ball with us. They find other people to play catch with or choose to play a different game (i.e., religion/values system) altogether.

As an illustration of this, there is a reason that most "nones" (i.e., adults who claim no faith) say that they lost their faith by age thirteen.[2] It has less to do with their religious formation than with the fact that their parents' faith failed to make a positive difference in the quality of their home life.[3] The fact that the parents of most "nones" didn't notice that their children had lost their faith until six years later, when the kids finally stop going to church as young adults, highlights the poor quality of relationships between parents and teens in many Christian households.

Whose Team Are You On?

It's no secret that the secular culture is unsupportive of many of the lessons Catholic parents want to pass on to their teens. As parents, when we encounter the music that our kids listen to, the movies and TV programs they watch, and the websites and apps they use, we can start to feel powerless. How can we possibly compete against a culture that is so opposed to the Christian way of life?

The good news is that while these things certainly play a role in shaping our teens, research consistently shows that the stronger the parent-child discipleship bond is, the healthier a teen's relationship will be with peers, media, and society as well.[4] By mastering the game of relationship "catch," Discipleship Parents can gently remind their teens that regardless of other influences, they are part of *God's* team *first*. To this end, Discipleship Parenting is entirely dependent upon your ability to build strong attachment with your adolescent.

Incline Your Heart to Me

Attachment is best understood as your teen's gut-level conviction (far beyond a merely intellectual appreciation) that you are the primary person to whom they can confidently and consistently turn for help in meeting their needs and living their best life. Attachment doesn't refer to how close you feel to your kids. It refers to how close your kids feel to you. Attachment is the measure of how confident your teen is that, whenever or however they throw the ball to you (i.e., communicate needs or express concerns), you will be able to catch it and throw it back well (i.e., help them meet those needs in godly, efficient, satisfying ways).

Again, secure attachment is not something that is cultivated solely in the infant and toddler years. Attachment is a continuum that extends through every stage of development, even into adulthood. Many parents engage in attachment parenting practices — such as extended nursing, babywearing, and sleep sharing — in infancy and toddlerhood and then think they have checked the attachment box. These practices are good, because they help parents respond promptly, generously, consistently, and cheerfully to the needs of infants and toddlers. But maintaining the attachment fostered through these early practices means continuing to meet the unique needs your child has at each stage of development (early childhood, middle childhood, pre-adolescence, and adolescence) in a similarly prompt, generous, consistent, and cheerful manner, as well as teaching them to respond in kind. "Doing attachment parenting" when children are infants and toddlers does not necessarily prevent parents and children from having poor attachment to their children later on. This approach essentially treats attachment parenting as a series of techniques you use on a child, instead of seeing it as a relationship you cultivate with your child. In order to maintain strong attachment over the years, Discipleship Parents must continue to attend to their children's developmental needs promptly, generously, consistently, and cheerfully through middle childhood and adolescence *and* teach their children how to respond in kind.

Parents who do not continue to build attachment throughout the preteen and teen years teach their children to turn to peers, media, and the culture to meet their needs, instead of Mom and Dad. In fact, failing to respond to the needs that accompany their child's later stages can effectively undermine the foundational attachment parents laid in the early years. It simply says to teens, "Mom and Dad are great at raising babies, but after I'm weaned, I'm supposed to figure everything else out for myself." Obviously, this can lead to some very serious problems. Attachment parenting practices in infancy are not a set of techniques parents use on their kids to guarantee successful outcomes later on. They are an invitation to an ongoing, deep, intimate relationship with the parent for years to come. Failing to continue the relationship initiated by attachment practices in the early years is like sending your child an invitation to a party and then slamming the door in their face when they show up.

Because attachment is a continuum, even if you never engaged in attachment-based parenting practices in the early years, it is not too late to start now. Although strong attachment is best served when the invitation to this ongoing, deep, and intimate relationship is extended from the parents to the child in the earliest years of their relationship, it is not too late to cultivate stronger attachment when your kids are tweens and teens, or even in adulthood. Every child wants to know that they are welcome to the party (i.e., a deep, intimate relationship with Mom and Dad) even if the invitation shows up later than they would have hoped for. We know forty-, fifty-, and sixty-year-olds who would give their right arm for a previously unattached parent to suddenly say, "I'm sorry I wasn't there for you the way you needed me before, but I am going to make sure that things are different from now on."

Tweens and teens who are not as securely attached as they could be will tend to be more resistant to parents' efforts to build relationship in the later years. They might wonder why they are being invited to the party now instead of years before. They may roll their eyes, huff and puff, and play hard to get. This is not because they don't want to be attached. It is because they are afraid to let you in. They need to know that your desire to build a deeper relationship isn't just some whim. They need to know that you are committed to the long haul. When a teen is used to a parent not responding to their needs promptly, generously, consistently, and cheerfully, they become afraid of opening their hearts. But in spite of this initial resistance, if you sustain your efforts to show your teen that you really do want to be the person who is most committed to helping them meet their needs in godly and effective ways, you will be surprised at how quickly their defenses come down. It is natural for tweens and teens to want strong attachment with their parents. Parents simply need to convincingly demonstrate that such a relationship is actually possible. In sum, whenever you are starting this process, it is never too late to foster stronger attachment with your kids. Your tweens and teens, especially, need to feel in their bones that they can turn to you for help in meeting the complicated needs and concerns they will be trying to address in the coming years.

Attachment Rule of Thumb

The best indication of how securely your teen is attached to you is the degree to which they are willing and able to accept your influence. That does not mean that a securely attached teen slavishly obeys every word that falls from your lips. Rather, a securely attached teen will be more likely to ask respectful questions and work through any objections or concerns they might have about what you're saying so that they can integrate the lessons you're trying to teach in ways that actually make sense for their life.

Attachment doesn't relate just to parent-child relationships, but also to friendships and romantic relationships as well. You know you are strongly attached to someone if you have a desire to be near them and accept their influence. You might say that you are strongly attached to someone if — more often than not — your first response to any situation is, "Even when I feel confident handling something myself, I enjoy sharing my experiences with so-and-so and seeking their help, support, and company." By contrast, you may be less attached to someone if you feel nervous about approaching them with your needs, worry about whether you can really count on them, or if it doesn't occur to you to approach them with your needs at all.

You've Got (Attachment) Style

Adolescence is all about learning how to have healthy relationships. The attachment style our parents cultivate with us ultimately informs the unconscious attitudes we have toward all relationships. Broadly speaking, a person may have a *secure* or *insecure* attachment style.

If you have a *secure attachment style,* you expect to be treated well, and you work hard to treat others well. You surround yourself with emotionally healthy, respectful, capable people who are good at giving and asking for support. Securely attached teens tend to be more resistant to the social drama (or, at the other extreme, the social isolation) that less well-attached teens are consumed by. Of course all adolescents get caught up in teen angst — this is unavoidable — but securely attached teens tend to be more resistant to it and recover from it more quickly. Similarly, it is rare for the securely attached teen to intentionally cause drama. In fact, they usually look for ways they can help their friends decrease the drama in their lives.

By contrast, the more *insecurely attached* you are, the more you tend to surround yourself with people who take advantage of you and are dismissive of your needs. In the extreme, the most insecurely attached people try to avoid needing or being needed by others at all. Insecurely attached teens tend to either create or unnecessarily insert themselves into the middle of relationship drama to feel needed and desired, or they avoid relationships altogether, preferring neither to need others or be needed by them.

The good news is that everyone can develop secure attachment. God created an entire part of our brain to support it. Researchers refer to the structures of the brain that support healthy attachment as the *social brain.* The neurological hardware of the social brain comes preinstalled at birth, but the software has to be uploaded — mainly by parents — throughout childhood and adolescence. Even if early opportunities to foster secure attachment are missed, people can learn to have healthier relationship styles later in life through a process called "earned secure attachment." Earned secure attachment occurs when people participate in healthy, warm relationships where the participants are expected to respond generously to one another. Earned secure attachment can occur between parents and older children, or even in relationships between adults who are striving to be consistently generous and kind to each other. Regardless of one's age, secure attachment is fostered when all the people in a relationship are expected to respond promptly, generously, consistently, and cheerfully to each other. This is, effectively, the dynamic Saint John Paul described when he wrote that healthy Christian relationships were distinguished by "mutual self-giving."

A host of studies going back to the late 1940s show that children develop secure attachment when parents respond promptly, generously, and consistently to their child's physical, emotional, relational, and spiritual needs. This prompt, generous, and consistent attention results in the child naturally turning toward the parents — physically, emotionally, and spiritually. The securely attached child views Mom and Dad as the primary sources for acquiring the nurturance and guidance he or she needs to flourish in life.[5]

This "turning toward" love represented by secure attachment is the basis for an authentic domestic-church-based spirituality. As Saint John Paul wrote in *Evangelium Vitae* ("The Gospel of Life"), "The celebration which gives meaning to every other form of prayer and worship is found in the family's actual daily life together, if it's a life of love and self-giving."[6]

This is the love we discussed at length in part one — the love that comes from the very heart of God and enables families to be icons of the Trinity and dynamic domestic churches. But what does it take to create the kind of relationship with your teens that makes them want to be not just your children but also your disciples?

The Evolution of Attachment

Attachment is a continuous process that must be fostered from infancy through young adulthood. It can be helped or hindered by how well parents deal with the needs and challenges a child expresses, not just in infancy, but at each stage of development. While a child's needs change from year to year, as long as parents continue to do their best to respond promptly, generously, and consistently to meet their child's needs and help their child be as generous as they are able in return, they will be doing what is necessary to foster strong attachment. For instance:

In the infant and toddler years, parents encourage secure attachment by responding promptly, generously, and consistently to their infant's and toddler's cries, and keeping their babies as physically close to their body as they reasonably can throughout the day and night.

In early childhood (ages three to six), parents foster attachment by taking time to teach their children the stories, rules, habits, and structures (i.e., routines and rituals) that facilitate a healthy way of life.

In middle childhood (ages six to ten), the parents foster strong attachment by helping their children manage school and peer challenges, discover their unique gifts and talents, and learn to use those gifts in positive ways. Through all this, the child learns how to be a functional, effective person.

In pre-adolescence (ages eleven to twelve) and adolescence (thirteen to nineteen), parents maintain strong attachment by helping their kids:

- identify and meet their needs in healthy, godly ways

- have healthy and meaningful relationships with peers
- discover ways to use their gifts to make a positive difference in the world

For adolescents, attachment-building practices are less physical than they are in infancy and childhood. Instead, these practices for preteens and teens are more psychological, emotional, relational, and spiritual. To maintain strong attachment with their child over the years, and especially through the tween and teen years, parents' behavior must send the message, "You can always turn to me — first and foremost — to get what you need to lead a healthy, godly, fulfilling life." Of course, most parents say this, but not all children actually *feel* it's true. The strength of the attachment the child feels predicts how likely it is that the child will open up when the parent invites him to do so.

It bears repeating that, in contrast to other parenting approaches, Discipleship Parenting isn't a series of techniques you employ with your child. It's an invitation to create a different kind of relationship with your child — a more intimate, interactive, and intentional relationship. Healthy consistency of caregiving (as opposed to either benign neglect or scrupulous perfectionism) combined with generous affection, a real willingness to listen, and gentle discipline throughout the various ages and stages of childhood are the keys to fostering the secure attachment that stands at the heart of a strong Discipleship Parenting bond.

Attachment on My Mind

As we've already suggested, our attachment style is more than a psychological or spiritual phenomenon. It carves itself into our brain. Research using functional imaging technology (fMRI, fPET) shows that consistent, healthy parental attachment behaviors literally stimulate growth in the child's *social brain*, the neurological seat of relational, emotional, and moral reasoning.[7] Other studies illustrate that poor parental attachment behaviors inhibit the development of the child's social brain, which, in turn, diminishes the child's capacity for intimacy, empathy, pro-social behavior, and healthy moral reasoning.

Daniel Siegel is a distinguished fellow of the American Psychiatric Association and world-renowned expert on parenting style's impact on brain development. He has an interesting Catholic connection too. In 1999, Pope Saint John Paul II asked Siegel to address the Pontifical Council on the Family — and the Holy Father personally — on the science of attachment. Siegel asserts that secure attachment is responsible for eight essential components of good mental health (see Table 1).[8]

Table 1: Secure Attachment Facilitates the Eight Components of Good Mental Health

1. Body Regulation	The ability to keep the body's systems (e.g., heart rate, respiration, body temperature) coordinated and balanced. This facilitates emotional health. *For example: A racing heart/respiration can precipitate anxiety. Feelings of exhaustion or under-stimulation can precipitate depression.*
2. Attuned Communication	The ability to pick up on nonverbal cues (facial expressions, tones of voice, posture) that indicate how other people are feeling/responding to you.
3. Emotional Balance	The ability to be emotionally stimulated enough to remain engaged without being flooded by feelings.
4. Response Flexibility	The ability to pause before acting on impulses and choose the best response to a situation. *People with ADHD, compulsive anger, addictions, and other impulse-control problems struggle with this skill.*
5. Fear Modulation	The ability to consciously turn down the volume on fearful feelings.

6. Insight	The ability to link my past, present, and future in a way that helps me make sense of my life and view myself in a compassionate manner.
7. Empathy	The ability to have insight (as defined above) into other people, to make sense of other people's lives, and view them with compassion.
8. Moral Reasoning	The ability to delay gratification, make healthy sacrifices for others, and act from the perspective of the greater good.

The more securely attached a person is, the more they're able to demonstrate the eight social brain-based skills that support good mental, relational, and spiritual health. By contrast, the more insecurely attached a person is, the more they will struggle to consistently exhibit some or all of the eight foundational mental health skills.

Feeling Insecure?

People who are insecurely attached fall into one of two basic categories: *anxious attachment* and *avoidant attachment.* The first type, anxious attachment, results when parents respond in a habitually delayed, reluctant, grudging, or inconsistent manner to their child's needs. Parents who adopt this attitude often worry about spoiling their children by being "too affectionate" or "too generous," particularly with their time and attention. These parents give their children the message that if they want love, approval, or real assistance they'll need to do something — get better grades, do more chores, etc. — to prove themselves worthy of their parents' investment in them. Such parents often point to the fact that their kids are high performers as "proof" that their approach is working. Unfortunately, these parents tend to be blind to the cost of this approach to success. Anxiously attached kids can grow up to be remarkably accomplished. They just never feel good about anything they do.

Returning to our analogy of discipleship as playing catch with our kids, parents who raise anxiously attached kids are either so busy lecturing their children about how to throw the ball properly that they never actually play the game (i.e., have a real relationship) or they're too distracted to consistently catch the balls the child throws to them — but then say it's the child's fault. This teen comes to believe that the game (i.e., relationship) doesn't go well because there's something wrong with *them*. If they only could try hard enough, they could finally make the game work the way it's supposed to.

Anxiously attached people are high-risk for scrupulosity/neurotic guilt, codependency, fears of abandonment, struggles with basic trust, poor self-care, anxiety disorders, substance abuse (particularly opioids), and the inappropriate use of affection/sex as a strategy to keep a romantic partner. While every teen or young adult dates some frogs on the way to finding their prince (or princess), insecurely attached teens and young adults tend to habitually (and perhaps exclusively) attach themselves to people who can't love them, and then blame themselves for the problems in the relationship.

Are You Avoiding Me?
The second type of insecure attachment, avoidant attachment, results from parents' miserly responses to their child's emotional and relational needs. Parents of avoidantly attached teens may not be — strictly speaking — abusive or neglectful, but they tend to be terminally disengaged and are often punitive, unaffectionate, intolerant of emotional displays, and allergic to anything that looks too much like "neediness."

Using the "playing catch" analogy, parents who raise avoidantly attached kids tend to refuse to give their kid a ball (i.e., cultivate a relationship) in the first place, telling them that it builds character to figure out how to get their own ball. If the child does manage to find a ball to toss to Mom or Dad (i.e., attempts to initiate connection), the parents duck it — usually because they're doing something "more important." After a while, the child just stops playing (i.e., relating in emotionally meaningful ways) and learns to look down on people who want to play on a team (i.e., be in an emotionally meaningful relationship) as being needy and unable to occupy themselves.

Avoidantly attached people tend to be suspicious of relationships and exhibit an unhealthy sense of autonomy, poor insight, and impaired empathy. They tend to be workaholics who prefer chasing accomplishment over close relationships with anyone. They often display a selfish (e.g., consumer- or power-based) approach to sex. They're also prone to anger control problems, substance abuse, and physical health complaints that are primarily caused by their inability to appropriately express needs and emotions.

God Attachment

Catholic parents have extra cause to be concerned about their child's attachment style. Research shows that a person's human attachment style usually corresponds very closely to their *God attachment style.*

Anxious God attachment leads people to view God as a punishing parent. Anxiously God attached Christians tend to feel that they're always at risk for wearing out God's love or trying his patience. They feel compelled to jump through hoops to try to win God's love.

By contrast, *avoidant God attachment* makes people either highly resistant to any relationship with God or relegates them to one that's rooted almost entirely in duty and rules over intimacy.[9]

In sum, a person's attachment style represents their unconscious, neurologically based inclination to turn toward or away from others and God. Without secure attachment, an individual's potential for achieving personal integration; healthy, emotionally deep, and rewarding human relationships; and an honest, intimate relationship with God is significantly compromised.

What About Me?

Some readers can get a little nervous at this point. Fear not. The good news is that even if you have an anxious or avoidant attachment style, it's possible to develop earned secure attachment. This is done by working hard to have healthy adult relationships and committing to an ongoing plan for personal/emotional/spiritual growth as adults. Again, using the playing catch analogy, even if you were taught all the wrong ways to throw, or even if you learned that playing catch was stupid, finding a person who could serve as a loving, supportive, patient coach would go a long way toward helping you learn to play the game properly (i.e., have healthy back-and-forth relationships).

If you have an anxious or avoidant attachment style, working to se-curely attach your own child can also be a very healing process. This is especially true if you make sure to get the support you need (including, when necessary, counseling) to deal with the sometimes surprising sense of resentment or anger that can emerge as you struggle with the feeling that *"No one ever gave me this kind of love or attention. How dare my child demand so much from me!"* Getting the support you need to move past this painful resistance is both worthwhile and deeply healing. We will discuss this process in greater detail in chapter 9.

The most important takeaway in this chapter is that fostering strong attachment with your children through every age and stage is the key to creating a discipleship relationship with your child. Strong attach-ment gives your child confidence that you can shepherd them toward a healthy, fulfilling, godly life. It makes your child resistant to unhealthy peer, media, and cultural influence. It makes your child want to listen to you, learn from you, and follow your lead without you having to resort to heavy-handed punishments and threats to get their attention.

Having explored the power of attachment to form healthy hearts and minds, the next chapter will look at how to use this power to build a House of Discipleship.

Prayer

Lord, help me to be your face of love to my children. Help me to attach my children's hearts to yours through the loving relationship I build with them day by day. Help me earn my children's trust at every stage and let them see me as their primary model for living a healthy, godly life. Make me a good disciple so I can raise my children to be even better disciples and follow you all their days of their lives.

Holy Family, pray for us! Amen.

Discussion Questions

Do you think you have more of a secure, anxious, or avoidant attach-ment style? What about your teen's attachment style?

Regardless of your attachment style, you can always develop more secure attachments. How did the information in this chapter challenge your attitudes toward relationships in general and parenting in particular?

What attachment style do you think you have been fostering in your children? Regardless of your answer, what do you think you could do to foster a stronger attachment bond with your children now that they have reached adolescence?

CHAPTER 8

Building a House of Discipleship

Parents have the first responsibility for the education of their children. They bear witness to this responsibility first by creating a home where tenderness, forgiveness, respect, fidelity, and disinterested service are the rule. The home is well suited for education in the virtues. This requires an apprenticeship in self-denial, sound judgment, and self-mastery — the preconditions of all true freedom.

CCC 2223

Every child needs secure attachment to thrive, but Discipleship Parenting takes the process of attachment one step further. Discipleship Parenting builds on strong attachment to accomplish two goals:

1. Give our kids a physical, bone-deep experience of the generous, extravagant love that comes from God's own heart.
2. Make our kids want to willingly turn to us to learn the lessons and skills they will need to live a truly loving, godly, fulfilling life in Christ.

These lessons become especially important in adolescence, when kids are learning what it means to love others, to meet their own needs in godly ways, and to find their place in the world.

We don't mean to suggest that other parents don't also want these things for their children. Of course they do. But there's a big difference between meaning to do something and actually doing it. Research consistently shows that parents are only able to disciple their teens into a healthy faith life and moral vision (i.e., one that's rooted in love rather than fear) to the degree that they are first able to foster at least some degree of secure attachment with their child. The opposite is also true. The more your teen resists your attempts to influence their faith or moral life, the more likely it is that they are not as securely attached to you as you need them to be. The good news is, there's a lot you can do to address this problem. We'll discuss ways to do this throughout this book, especially in the chapters on developmental stages.

The House of Discipleship

Raising godly children is not primarily an intellectual exercise, but a relational one. At each stage of a child's development, Discipleship Parents use the strong attachment they foster with their children as the construction materials they need to build a warm, loving, grace-filled House of Discipleship.

As you can see in the House of Discipleship graphic, ideally, Discipleship Parents begin the process of raising godly, healthy children by helping their infants and toddlers learn how to regulate their bodily reactions and impulses, fostering the physical and neurological basis for trust, self-control, and empathy. These qualities become brain-based building blocks for faith and moral reasoning.[1]

Next, in early childhood, Discipleship Parents help their kids develop the foundations of a Christian worldview by establishing a loving environment in which the stories, rules, and structures that make up an orderly, peaceful life can be learned.

In middle childhood, Discipleship Parents plant the seeds of their child's future vocation by helping their child develop their unique gifts and talents. They also help their children learn to use their gifts to both make meaningful contributions to family life and have a pos-

House of Discipleship

Stage Four: Relational Discipleship (Adolescence)

Teen turns toward parent to develop skills for having godly relationships and finding place in world.

Stage Three: Vocational Discipleship (Middle Childhood)

Child turns toward parent to discover and develop gifts in a way that helps him glorify God and make meaningful contributions to family and others.

Stage Two: Foundational Discipleship (Early Childhood)

Child turns toward parent to learn the stories, rules, and structures that lead to a love-filled, well-ordered life.

Stage One: Embodied Discipleship (Infancy and Toddlerhood)

Child turns toward parent to learn self-regulation and empathy through body-to-body communication.

itive impact on their peers.

Finally, in adolescence, Discipleship Parents show teens how their faith and moral vision can help them develop healthy, meaningful, godly relationships and discover God's plan for their place in the world.

Although it is ideal that parents would begin this discipleship relationship in the earliest years of their child's life, the strong attachment that makes Discipleship Parenting possible can be built at any stage. It may simply require a bit more effort to break through a preteen's or teen's initial resistance if they aren't used to relating to you on this level. Try not to get angry if your preteen or teen doesn't immediately respond to your efforts to create a stronger bond. This kind of mentoring relationship isn't just a duty the child owes you. It is mainly a connection that must be cultivated by you. Although we owe obedience to God, our heavenly Father doesn't wait for us to come to him. He runs to meet us on the road (see Lk 15:20). Discipleship Parents seek to follow the Father's example by not simply demanding or assuming a relationship with our children, but rather eagerly pursuing that relationship.

By lovingly investing our time in our children and cultivating an open-hearted attitude toward our children, Discipleship Parents send the message, "I am committed to helping you meet your (physical, psychosocial, relational) needs in a way that will satisfy you and keep you on a godly path." This is the message that will keep your child turning toward you even as his needs become more complicated and his social network expands.

A discipleship relationship is possible between parents and children at every age and stage of your child's development. And this is exactly the kind of relationship the Church's theology of family intends parents to cultivate within their homes.

Attachment is the single most important tool you have in your toolbox. Everything else depends upon it. The effectiveness of any discipline approach (ours or anyone else's) is directly dependent upon the strength of attachment between parents and children. The weaker the attachment bond, the more children push back against their parents' guidance and the more parents are forced to rely on lecturing, yelling, and heavy-handed, punishment-based strategies to compel their teenagers to listen to them. This latter approach is common enough — even in many

Catholic households. Even so, this approach is completely inconsistent with our call to follow the example of the Good Shepherd as we patiently and gently lead our little sheep to the Father.

What It's NOT...

Discipleship Parenting vs. Spoiling

As we wrap up this chapter, it's important to offer a few words of clarification. First, many people express the concern that responding "promptly, generously, and consistently" to their teens will make them narcissistic and selfish and, in essence, spoil them. This is an understandable concern, especially for Christian parents. Let's reflect on what spoiling a child at any age actually means.

Popularly, people think "spoiling" is the same as being generous. Not only is this psychologically wrongheaded, it's directly contrary to how every Christian is called to live. Remember, the Church teaches that we become fully human by challenging ourselves to be more generous to others (see *Gaudium et Spes*). Likewise, we are called to follow God's example, and God is immeasurably generous. In fact, God is so generous that the psalmist tells us that he starts responding before our prayer leaves our mouths (Ps 139:4). Repeatedly throughout the Gospels, Christ generously gives more than people can possibly receive: more wine than is needed, more loaves than anyone knows what to do with, more fish than the nets can hold. The Christian God created an entire universe that most of us will never see, just in case we might one day want to explore it. The Christian God is ridiculously, insanely extravagant in his providence, love, mercy, and grace. As Christians, we're called to be similarly generous. Reflecting on our heavenly Father's example, we see that it's more than possible to be incredibly generous to our teenagers without spoiling them.

Our kids aren't spoiled because we are generous to them. They are spoiled when we are generous without requiring them to give back as much as they're capable at each age and stage. This is exactly the model Christ uses. Jesus gives us his whole self freely — but heaven isn't free. It's only open to those who respond to Jesus' invitation and give themselves totally back to him. In a similar way, relationships between any two people — especially parents and children — only thrive when both people in that relationship are doing everything they can to give 100 percent to each other. Saint John Paul referred to this as "mutual self-donation." Mutual self-donation is the dynamic that exists between any group of people who consistently challenge themselves to promptly, generously, and consistently respond to one another's needs so that everyone in the relationship is able to flourish. This is the basis for the civilization of love that Saint John Paul said it was every Christian's duty to create.

We don't flourish by being stingy. Misers don't live abundant lives. Neither do we prevent our adolescents from being spoiled and selfish by being stingy with them. In fact, deprivation is exactly what causes a selfish, grasping, self-protective attitude in teens and adults.

Discipleship Parents strive to be heroically generous to their children, but they avoid spoiling their children by requiring them to give back to the family and to others as much as they're able as they grow and mature. As the child matures into adolescence and young adulthood, Discipleship Parents continue to respond as generously as they can to their child's needs while helping the child take on more responsibilities around the house and challenging the child to be as generous to his siblings, friends, and the community as Mom and Dad have tried to be to him.

Needs vs. Wants

Often parents of teens are either intimidated or completely put off by the idea of responding promptly, generously, and consistently to their teens' needs. "It sounds like you're saying we have to give our teens everything they want."

That's not what we're saying at all. Even so, it does require parents to think differently about what constitutes a need and a want and how to appropriately help our teens meet both.

Most parents define *needs* as anything related to basic survival (food, shelter, safety), while *wants* refer to the preferences or whims that help us live more comfortably. When a child comes to us with a request that isn't concerned with meeting their basic needs, especially if it makes us uncomfortable in some way (maybe we're suspicious of the benefits of that thing, or we can't afford it, or we aren't sure the child can handle it), we simply dismiss their request by saying, "No. You don't need that!" There are certainly times we will need to say no to our children, but taking the above approach tends to undermine our attachment to our teens because it sends the message that they can expect to be shamed by us if they haven't figured out exactly what they need and how to ask for it.

A better approach is to understand needs as the things that we require to function at our best. This goes far beyond basic needs like food, shelter, and safety, and includes things like respect, acceptance, enjoyment, and fulfillment. By contrast, a want isn't a lesser need that we can respond to only if it pleases us. It is simply the preferred way to meet a need. It can be hard to tell the difference between wants and needs. It's part of a Discipleship Parent's job to teach their teens to do just that. Kids often lead with a want that's confused with a need. They need our help to identify the need behind the want and then figure out healthy ways to meet the need. For instance, imagine that your teen asks for something you think is out of the question (e.g., a particularly violent video game or $500 sneakers). Your natural tendency might be to simply say no to the superficial request for the inappropriate thing. That's certainly understandable, but it may be missing the point — especially if it results in an argument between you and your teen. A better approach is to stop and say, "Hmmm. Can you tell me more about what getting that thing would do for you?"

Asking this question gets at the need behind the want. In the conversation that follows, you might discover that your teen is really struggling to know how to fit in to a particular group that is important to them, or succeed in an environment you put them in. As you talk through things, you might realize that your teen doesn't really care if they get the thing they asked you for. Rather, they are seeking help in discerning how to make their life and relationships work. If you shut down the conversation by simply screaming, "You want WHAT?!? Are you out of your mind?!?" you've undermined attachment. On the other hand, by saying, "Help me understand what you think getting that would do for you?" you've taken the time to help your teen identify their real need, and you've opened up the door for many other conversations. In the process, you have set up a dynamic where you have confirmed to your child that they can come to you with any request and expect a fair hearing. They may not always get what they ask for at first, but they can always count on you to help them figure out what they really need and how to get that.

This is the essence of the prompt, generous, consistent response that stands at the heart of Discipleship Parenting. We'll explore more ways to practice this skill in the chapters on discipleship discipline and developmental stages.

Discipleship Parenting vs. Helicopter and Rapunzel Parenting

As we continue to explore what Discipleship Parenting is not, it's worth taking a moment to compare Discipleship Parenting with helicopter parenting and what we will call "Rapunzel parenting." These latter approaches are very different from healthy Discipleship Parenting.

Helicopter Parenting

In addition to providing skills and support, Discipleship Parents are invested in giving teens the space they need to struggle and succeed in a supportive environment. By contrast, helicopter parents tend to focus on telling their teens what to do, but they never give them an opportunity to do it — much less the space they need to do it independently. Helicopter parenting is really an anti-discipleship relationship based in fear, not love. Helicopter parents are always around, but their presence fosters anxious attachment. They are so busy telling their teen all the rules for throwing the ball (and all the things that could go wrong) that they never allow the child to actually play. That makes kids nervous when it's their turn at bat.

This doesn't mean that Discipleship Parents are content to let their kids fail classes, get drunk, or engage in premarital sex, etc., because they need to "learn a lesson." But it does mean that, having had the "Can you tell me what getting that/doing that would do for you?" conversation we discussed above, a parent might let their teen dye their hair an unusual color, wear a particular article of clothing, go to a particular event, or engage in an activity that, while not being objectively immoral, was certainly a stretch to the parent's comfort zone. Part of being an effective Discipleship Parent is making it safe to make mistakes. "Safe mistakes" are those that allow the child to fail without risking seriously life-altering consequences.

What we call "Rapunzel parenting" is another thing that parents confuse with Discipleship Parenting. Again, certain well-meaning Catholic parents believe that if — like the witch in the story "Rapunzel" — they can just keep their teen away from all influences that could compete with their own authority as parents, they will succeed in raising godly children. As the Rapunzel story illustrates, however, the opposite is more often true. Like helicopter parenting, Rapunzel parenting is also an anti-discipleship, fear-based relationship. Returning to our "playing catch" metaphor, Rapunzel parents allow their child to watch classic sports TV shows with the promise that if the child is attentive enough, one day they will learn to be great catchers too. Unfortunately, this approach often results in a moralistic person who knows how everything "should" be, but can't actually cope with the messiness of real life.

Parents who are tempted toward Rapunzel parenting need to understand the difference between naivete and true innocence. Naivete is simple ignorance of a bad thing. True innocence is the ability to encounter a bad thing and still be able to be good and live gracefully. The fact that your teen was exposed to something (or even sought out something) that you feel is inappropriate is not a catastrophe. That song, movie, website, or experience may have made them less naive, but it will not take their innocence if you use the opportunity to have a conversation (NOT lecture) with them about what was good about that thing, what was bad about it, what it meant to them, what they liked or didn't like about it, and how they think that thing either helps or potentially hinders their ability to be the person God is calling them to be. This conversation will be even more productive if you have had the discussions about mission that we referenced in the chapters discussing family life as a ministry and discipleship discipline.

In our professional experience, helicopter and Rapunzel parents are motivated by the fear that their child's mistakes will reflect poorly on them. Helicopter and Rapunzel parents are so overly concerned about others' judgment of them that they are afraid to put their children in situations where their lessons could be tested and honed.

The alternative to either helicopter or Rapunzel parenting is *not* simply letting the child struggle through the school of hard knocks on their own. Rather, it is *discipling* the child into success just like Saint John Bosco taught. Discipleship Parents provide the skills, support, and space their teens need to learn self-mastery and success in an environment where it's safe to make and learn from mistakes. Finding this balance can be challenging. It looks a little different with every child. We will give you guideposts throughout this book to help you find your way.

Prayer

Lord, please open my heart wide to my teens. Let them find you looking out at them through my eyes, and experience your love pouring out of my heart. Help me to draw them close to me so that I can ultimately lead them to you. Make me as generous to them as you are to me and let my example inspire them to work for the good of our household and all the people you place in their path as they grow into godly adults. May the love that comes from your heart shine out through my family and draw all the world to you.

Holy Family, pray for us. Amen.

Questions for Reflection

How does the idea of Discipleship Parenting challenge your idea of what it means to be a Catholic parent?

When you were a teen, in what ways did your parents practice at least some aspects of Discipleship Parenting? Were their efforts to get you to turn toward them and listen to them rooted in love or fear? How might your preteen and teen years have been different if your parents had used the ideas we describe in this chapter?

How do the ideas outlined in this chapter compare to your current relationship with/attitude toward your preteens/teens? What might change if you were to begin using more of these ideas in your relationship with your child?

CHAPTER 9

The Healing Power of Discipleship Parenting

*By calling God "Father," the language of faith ... thus
draws on the human experience of parents, who are in
a way the first representatives of God for man. But this
experience also tells us that human parents are fallible and
can disfigure the face of fatherhood and motherhood.*

CCC 239

*By knowing how to acknowledge their own failings to their
children, parents will be better able to guide and correct them.*

CCC 2223

*I will give you a new heart, and a new spirit I will
put within you. I will remove the heart of stone
from your flesh and give you a heart of flesh.*

Ezekiel 36:26

Very few of us came out of our own teen years unscathed. Discipleship Parenting isn't only about attending to our kids. It is also about understanding how God uses our parenthood to heal the wounds we all carry inside that make it difficult to receive the love our heavenly Father wants to give us.

The Struggle Is Real

As you try to apply the suggestions in this book, you may be surprised to find your own woundedness sometimes getting in the way. Maybe you feel stressed or anxious. Perhaps you feel cynical, irritated, or resentful. Maybe you find yourself being drawn into constant power struggles with your teen that have every bit as much to do with your emotional triggers as your kid's stubbornness. Maybe there's even a part of you that resists the idea of creating a truly intimate discipleship bond with your teen because it feels strange, forced, or somehow unnatural or even wrong. These feelings don't mean that there is something uniquely wrong with you. They just mean you're human. Even so, the more we give into these reactions, the harder it is for us to experience parenting as the healing experience God wants it to be *for us*. The struggles you encounter as you attempt to practice Discipleship Parenting are not the result of some personality issue that you simply have to accept. They are evidence of a spiritual wound that God wants to heal.

Made for Love

We were all created for love. As God's children, we're destined to spend eternity in a loving, intimate communion with God and all the saints. Unfortunately, sin can make even the idea of this intimate, close communion seem foreign. That's why God wants us to spend our time on earth learning how to be as fully intimate as we can with the people who share our lives — especially our children. Remember what Jesus said: "Amen, I say to you, unless you turn and become like children, you will not enter the kingdom of heaven" (Mt 18:3).

The more we work to create this intimate connection — especially with our spouse and children — the more healed and fully human we become *and* the more we prepare ourselves to share in our heavenly destiny. Discipleship Parenting is ultimately a healing enterprise because it is an education in the kind of self-giving love that makes us whole and holy.

It's true that Discipleship Parenting may come more naturally to some parents than others, but it involves challenges for everyone. Learning to love ourselves and our teens with the love that comes from God's heart is hard work! That said, any struggle or resistance we may encounter in maintaining a securely attached discipleship relationship with our kids is not due to the way we "are." It's due to the way we were hurt. The struggles we experience in nurturing a strong attachment/discipleship relationship with our children through adolescence are usually related to how much our own parents struggled to help us meet our emotional, relational, or spiritual needs when we were teens. Our heavenly Father wants to heal those wounds. He wants to meet those needs. The heart-to-heart connection Discipleship Parenting seeks to create between God, you, and your child allows the Lord's healing grace to fill the empty, dark spaces that are sometimes uncovered when we're trying to give our children the love God wants them to have. Remember God's promise: "I will give you a new heart, and a new spirit I will put within you. I will remove the heart of stone from your flesh and give you a heart of flesh" (Ez 36:26). God wants to fulfill this promise through the ministry of parenting in your domestic church.

The Parent Trap: Work vs. Toil

The world tells us that parenting teens is meant to be a thankless, exhausting, frustrating task. Many Catholic parents we have encountered seem to believe, at least implicitly, that parenting is only holy to the degree that it is hard and miserable. In light of these messages, it can be difficult to believe that parenting could be a source of anything except migraines.

We're not saying that parenting at any stage — *especially* in the preteen and teen years — is easy. We also don't mean to suggest that if you feel tired, frustrated, resentful, or angry some days, and even several days at a time — that there is something wrong with you or your kids. There isn't. Every parent experiences this from time to time.

Yet, if every day feels like drudgery … if you are in a constant battle with your adolescents … if you feel perpetually drained, resentful, angry, or depleted … please know this is not what parenting — especially Discipleship Parenting — is meant to be. These feelings are clear signs that there is a need for deeper healing. Being a parent is hard work, but it's not meant to feel like a rock around your neck.

There is a difference between hard work and what is called "toil." The Book of Genesis reminds us that Adam and Eve were created to tend the Garden of Paradise. But before the Fall, when God, humankind, and creation existed in a harmonious relationship with each other, the work our first parents did was joyful. Adam and Eve rejoiced in the ways God worked through them.

It was only after the Fall, when the relationship between God, humankind, and creation was shattered, that their work became *toil*. Toil is work that's mind-numbing, exhausting, and devoid of any sense of satisfaction or divine purpose. "Another day, another list of thankless, tiresome tasks." Does this sound like the way a lot of parents you know approach child-rearing? Maybe it even describes how you feel. If so, the good news is, there is a way out of this parenting trap.

The Way Out

Saint John Paul's Theology of the Body reminds us that for work to feel life-giving, it has to be *relational*. We have to do our work in a manner that keeps us connected to God, others, and our best selves.

Parenting preteens and teens is hard work, but it's only draining and soul-crushing toil if we give in to the temptation to see adolescence as a trial to be borne and our teens as either projects to be managed, juvenile delinquents to be wary of, or tests we have to pass to prove our worth. As soon as we start thinking this way, the work of parenting becomes toil, and we start to burn out. The good news? When we focus on creating a discipleship relationship with our preteens and teens, the hard work of parenting becomes a source of joy and healing. We experience God working in us, through us, and with us. Together with God's grace, we can make our homes into graceful spaces filled with warmth and love — even when the going gets tough.

Here are some ways you can begin to unpack the healing power of Discipleship Parenting.

Release Your Priestly Power – Consecrate Every Moment

We unlock the healing power of Discipleship Parenting by consecrating every moment to Christ — good, bad, painful, joyful, and otherwise. That's more than a pious sentiment. It's a practical exercise for tapping into sacramental, healing grace. Here's how it works.

Through our baptism, we are initiated into the common priesthood. While it's the job of the ministerial priesthood to administer all the sacraments and, in particular, to consecrate the bread and the wine into the Body and Blood of Christ, it's the job of the common priesthood (i.e., baptized laypeople) to consecrate the world to Christ. As we discussed in the very first chapter, Discipleship Parents need to invite God into every good, bad, and ugly moment of our domestic church life. When we do this, we consecrate these moments and make them a source of grace and healing. Through our running conversation with God, we practice listening to his voice speaking through each moment and telling us how to respond to that moment in a way that helps us become the whole, healed, godly, grace-filled people we're meant to be.

As common priests exercising the ministry of parenthood and witnessing to Christ's sacrificial love, we become a bridge between God and our kids.[1] God uses us as an instrument for filling our hearts, our homes, and our kids with this love.

The love we have for our children doesn't start with us. It actually comes from God and flows through us. You can tap into the healing power of this love as it flows through you. Even though adolescence can be tough on parents and kids, every parent experiences some moments when they feel close to their teen. In that moment, close your eyes. Imagine that the love that you feel for your child is being poured into your heart by your heavenly Father. Look into your Father's eyes. See that the love you have for your teen is just a fraction of the love God has for you — a tiny portion of the love God is pouring into your heart. Take a moment to revel in that love. Let it soak in. Offer up a brief prayer consecrating that moment to God. *Lord, I praise you for your abundant love. Fill up every part of me with your love and grace. Help me to never doubt my worth in your eyes and help me be a perfect channel of your love for my kids.*

In addition to this simple exercise, try to keep two questions in mind throughout your day. First, ask yourself, "How can I use this parenting moment to try to become a tiny bit more of the whole, healed, godly, grace-filled person God wants me to be?"

Second, when you struggle to be that whole, healed, godly, grace-filled person, ask yourself, "How can I let my limitations invite me to rely more on God's mercy and grace?" Remember, we need to be pleased to be works in progress. As God told Saint Paul, "My grace is sufficient for you, for power is made perfect in weakness" (2 Cor 12:9). Let God's grace fill the gaps you can't fill with your own energy.

Through these priestly acts of consecrating every moment to God and modeling Christ's sacrificial love the best you can, you release the healing power of your domestic church.

Release Your Prophetic Power – State Your Needs

In addition to your priestly mission, you were given a prophetic mission in baptism. We live out the prophetic mission of our baptism by showing others how to live the Faith in the real world (see CCC 785). One of the ways parents do this is by showing our kids — through our example — how to have a healthy relationship with our God-given needs.

Having a healthy relationship with our God-given needs doesn't mean either ignoring them or being bossy about them. It means meeting them in ways that give glory to God, respect the needs of others, and help us become the people we were created to be.

God made you. He also made your needs. Your needs tell the story of how God made you not only to survive, but to thrive. You *must* make sure your needs for nutrition, hygiene, respect, relationship, spiritual connection, and growth are being met. You can't do this all by yourself. You need help. Needing help doesn't mean you're an insufficient parent. It means you are functioning exactly the way God made you to function. Part of the reason God gave us needs is so that we would be inspired to turn to him and others for help. God expects us to bring our needs to each other. That's how we build the "communities of love" Saint John Paul talked about.

And here's something that often comes as a surprise to readers. God wants you to *expect* that the people in your life will help you meet your needs every bit as much as you help them meet theirs. It's not supposed to be all up to you. You have a right to expect your spouse and your kids

— especially your teens — to help make your home the orderly, peaceful, loving, joyful, supportive haven it's meant to be. This is Saint John Paul's idea of "mutual self-donation" at work. It's mutual self-donation that makes relationships healthy, strong, and satisfying.

This is lost on a lot of parents, especially those with insecure attachment. Everyone has at least some difficulty telling other people their needs. It feels vulnerable and a little bit scary. But for people with an anxious attachment style, the very idea of having needs feels like a sin, never mind expecting others to help meet those needs. Likewise, people with avoidant attachment are barely aware that they have needs, much less willing to admit them to anyone else.

Teens have lots of needs. Discipleship Parenting is about helping our kids turn to us at every age and stage so that we can show them — by word and example — how to meet all their needs in godly, efficient ways. Teaching our kids to live abundant, godly lives is the prophetic ministry of parenthood, but we can't teach our teens godly ways to meet their needs if we aren't doing it ourselves.

As human beings, we suffer when we don't tell others what we need. Some Catholics have the mistaken impression that suffering automatically makes us holy. It doesn't. It's our *response* to suffering that makes us holy, and the only holy response to suffering is compassion. We must always do what we can to address the causes of suffering — to meet the need, address the concern, heal the wound. We must be compassionate to our own needs and the needs of others. As Jesus said, "Love your neighbor *as yourself*." Discipleship Parents must learn to be compassionate toward the suffering of both their children and themselves.

If you feel guilty telling others what you need or getting others to take your needs seriously, these are serious problems that can undermine your mental health, the quality of your family life, and your ability to live your prophetic witness as a discipleship parent. We would like to gently encourage you to seek help in overcoming this struggle. Although there is more to this process than we can adequately address in these pages, you might find two of Greg's books helpful: *God Help Me! These People Are Driving Me Nuts* (which is about learning to be gracefully assertive) and *Unworried: A Life Without Anxiety* (which discusses how to fight anxiety by effectively meeting one's physical, emotional, relational, and spiritual needs). You may also learn more about the pastoral tele-counseling services we offer through CatholicCounselors.com if you would like more personal assistance.

Regardless of where you stand with this skill, finding godly ways to meet your needs while attending generously to the needs of others is an important way of exercising your prophetic mission and releasing the healing power of your domestic church.

Release Your Royal Power – Engage

Finally, in addition to the priestly and prophetic missions, we're also given a royal mission in baptism. We fulfill our royal mission by serving those around us with the love of Christ (see CCC 786). It isn't enough to serve to get things done. We must serve with godly love. This is an especially important thing to model for our teens, who often forget that doing chores, keeping up with assignments, and being responsible and respectful aren't just "things they have to do," but also important ways to say "I love you."

Discipleship Parents exercise their royal mission not just by doing the tasks involved in keeping family life running smoothly (cleaning, cooking, maintaining, paying bills, etc.), but also by trying to do them in a way that draws our kids closer to us and God. The following chart illustrates impoverished attitudes that undermine our royal mission in parenting versus healthy attitudes that support it.

Impoverished Attitude	Royal Attitude
When doing a task, I tend to push others out of the way because they always do it "wrong" and it's easier to do it myself.	When doing a task, I look for ways to include my kids so they can learn to help and serve.
I tend to rush around from task to task and struggle to find the time or energy to connect with my kids.	I try to pace myself when doing household tasks so that I can still talk/be present to my kids while I work.

I often feel put-upon or resentful about the things I have to do for my kids (and it probably shows).	Even when it's hard, I make an honest effort to do things for my kids in a way that communicates God's love for them.
I tend to feel like the things I do to take care of my family are more of a bother than a blessing.	I do my best to remember that the things I do to take care of my family mean a lot to them and make an important difference in their lives.
I'm frustrated that I never seem to get enough "me time" and, when I do, I hate coming back.	I take breaks when I need them, but I also get real joy from maintaining both my home and relationship with my kids.
I am much happier serving people outside my home than in it.	I enjoy my family and see them as my primary ministry. I only say yes to outside activities if they don't compete with my ability to be present to my family.

The point of this checklist isn't to judge any parent who identifies more with the sentiments on the left rather than those on the right. It's simply to note that parents who work hard to cultivate the attitudes on the right tend to experience more life satisfaction in general, and get more joy out of parenting in particular. Sometimes, even the best parents have a difficult time maintaining these more positive attitudes. While it's important to do what you can to view your parenthood through this healthier lens, and sometimes it's necessary to "fake it till you make it," this effort shouldn't feel perpetually forced or phony. If, despite your best attempts, you just can't bring yourself to break free of these more impoverished views toward family service, it might indicate that you are struggling with an attachment wound that requires professional help to heal — not just for your own benefit, but also because you can't give what you don't have. Discipling teens means teaching them what it takes to lead their own healthy families some day. If you want your kids to grow up to have joyful, generous, supportive families, you have to witness ways to do it.

Impoverished attitudes toward parenting are quite common for people with anxious and avoidant attachment styles. The good news is, these impoverished views don't represent an immutable personality type. They aren't the way you are; they point to the ways you were hurt. Becoming aware of this opens up pathways for healing.

Ultimately, the more we lean into our royal mission as parents, the more we become resistant to burnout. *Burnout = Effort - Meaning*. The more we approach parenting as a series of thankless, neverending tasks that have nothing to do with relationship, the more we feel like cogs instead of people, and the more burned-out we become.

Many burned-out parents try to recharge by getting away. Of course, knowing when to take timely breaks is an important survival skill for every parent, especially if you use some of your time away to make a plan to address the problems causing your stress in the first place. But research on burnout suggests that leaning too heavily on time away can actually increase our overall sense of dissatisfaction.[2] Although getting away can feel good, you always have to go back again — usually to a bigger pile of stuff to do.

A more effective strategy for beating burnout is recharging your sense of meaning through *the practice of presence*. Essentially, this involves being more thoughtful and intentional about whatever you're doing. Making dinner? Think about *why* you're cooking — how each bite of food makes your kids stronger and helps them grow into the people they were created to be. Tidying up? Think about *why* you're cleaning — taking care of the things you've been given is a way of saying "thank you" to God for his generosity and love. Doing a fun activity with your kids? Focus on really connecting with their smiles. Teens don't smile easily — especially with Mom and Dad. Make sure to praise God for the gift of your teen's joy when they share it with you. While you're at it, thank God for the reminder that it's okay to be a little silly yourself.

Our book *The Corporal Works of Mommy (and Daddy Too!)* can help you reengage your sense of meaningfulness by showing you how to connect with the grace hiding just below the surface of all the things you do all day. Embracing the royal mission of baptism heals our hearts by helping us serve others out of a sense of genuine love and divine purpose.

Two Powerful Techniques

In addition to receiving the healing that comes from embracing the priestly, prophetic, and royal dimensions of Discipleship Parenthood, there are two powerful techniques that anyone can use to untap the healing power of their domestic church: namely, the Four Questions Technique and the Inside Out Exercise.

Four Questions Technique

Many of the struggles we face in creating strong attachments with our kids are rooted in unhealthy attitudes we learned in our families of origin. Healing these wounds requires us to become aware of the unconscious scripts that drive our actions so that we can intentionally redirect our emotional energy down healthier paths.

Every parent occasionally responds to their kids in ways that they regret after the fact but feel powerless to change in the moment. The Four Questions Technique can help you develop productive responses to your children's problem behaviors. When you feel disappointed in yourself for reacting poorly to your teen, write out your reflections to the following four questions:

1. How did my mom and/or dad approach situations like this?
2. As a child, did their approach draw me closer to them or make me afraid and close off to them?
3. Would I want my child to feel the same way toward me as I did toward my parent in this situation? If not, how would I like them to feel toward me?
4. How might I need to change my approach so that I can effectively address this problem, but still allow my child to feel the way I would have wanted to feel toward my mom and/or dad?

Here are a few examples of how parents have used this exercise to address the wounds that made it difficult for them to be their best selves with their kids:

Alan, a forty-year-old father of three (ages fifteen, twelve, and ten), often found himself getting angry with his son, Jacob (fifteen) and daughter Michelle (twelve). He didn't have as many issues with Tammy (ten) because she was still at an age where she would do what she was told most of the time. But as the kids got older and either expressed more resistance or questioned why they had to do certain things, Alan felt that they were challenging his authority. Power struggles were becoming habitual. He would regularly find himself screaming at his kids to the point that there was constant tension in the household. Finally, his wife, Bethany, told Alan that she couldn't take it anymore. He would either need to get help for his reactions or she was going to divorce him. He agreed to come to family counseling, but he continued to insist that although he didn't like having to yell at his kids, they "made him do it" because of their constant disobedience and disrespect.

Alan related a recent situation in which he asked Jacob to shut down his video game and come to dinner. He said that his son ignored him, so he began yelling at the boy, lecturing him on the need to be respectful. Jacob responded by throwing the game controller across the room, storming out, and slamming the door of his room. Things got ugly from there as Alan, enraged at his son's disrespect, got up in his son's face. He swore at him repeatedly and took the door off the hinges of his son's room, telling him he could have it back when he "stopped acting like a little sh**."

We asked Alan, "How did your dad approach situations like this?" **(Question 1)**

Alan said, "My dad would never tolerate the way my kids behave."

"Really? What would he do?"

"If we didn't listen the first time, he would get up in our face and let us know that if we didn't get to it right then, he would make our lives miserable." Alan shook his head. "The one or two times that we pushed it past that point, things got physical. I remembered one time he slapped me so hard for talking back to him that my jaw hurt for a week. You definitely did not cross my dad."

"What did you do after your dad hit you like that?"

Alan chuckled nervously at the memory. "I hated him. But I did what he said. It was his house. His rules."

"So, it looks like your dad found a way to get you to listen to him, but did your dad's approach make you feel closer to him? Or did it make you afraid of him or want to close off to him?" **(Question 2)**

"I mean, look. I knew my dad loved me. He was tough, and he had his moments, but he was a really good dad. He sacrificed a lot for us. He had a right to expect me to respect him."

"I don't disagree that he loved you, and I know you've said how much you respect him even now. But did the way he handled these kinds of situations make you feel closer to him, or did it make you afraid of him?"

"Well, we were close in lots of different ways, but I was definitely afraid then."

"Would you want your kids to feel the same way about you as you did your dad in those times?" **(Question 3)**

"You mean, do I want them to be afraid of me?"

"Yes."

"Well, I want them to respect me."

"Of course, but do you want them to be afraid of you the same way you felt afraid of your dad in those times?"

Alan hesitated a moment and then shook his head. "No. Like I said, I want my kids to respect me, but I would never want them to be afraid of me. Sometimes, when I walk into the room, everyone gets quiet. Like I've sucked all the air out of the room. It makes me feel like a villain. I really hate that."

"Alan, if we could find some ways to get your kids to respect you without you having to make them afraid of you, would that be okay?" **(Question 4)**

Alan became very quiet and thoughtful. "I'm feeling a little choked up right now. Sorry. I love my dad, and I know he loved me too, but I don't want to make my kids feel about me the way I felt about him. I stopped talking to him for years after I got out of college. It took a long time for me to want to be around him as an adult. It would kill me if my kids ever felt that way about me. It would be good to have some ways to get their respect without having to make them afraid of me."

We inherit a lot of scripts from our parents. When our kids push our buttons, we react. We remember that what our parents did "worked," in that it made us do what they wanted us to do. In the moment, that looks like the answer we've been searching for and we latch on to it. Sometimes that's a good thing. Sometimes, not so much.

Going through the Four Questions Technique forces us to think a little bit deeper — to appreciate that our ends don't always justify our means. Every exchange we have with our kids makes them either open up or close off a little bit. Any single exchange doesn't make that much of a difference in the overall picture. But when an exchange becomes a pattern and the pattern defines the relationship, that's another thing altogether.

Leading Alan through the Four Questions Technique made him realize that he was losing his teens' hearts. He connected with the fact that even though he always loved and respected his father, he never really felt close to his dad. He was determined to create a different kind of relationship with his own kids. That decision didn't just make him a better dad; it also allowed him to begin healing the attachment wound at the heart of his anger.

Here's another example:

Jyllian and her sixteen-year-old daughter, Meghan, were constantly battling. Meghan complained that Jyllian "never lets me do anything."

For her part, Jyllian didn't trust Meghan. "She won't tell me anything. If I ask her about her day or what she plans on doing, she either refuses to talk to me or gives me one-word answers. If she wasn't doing something bad, why wouldn't she just answer my questions?"

In session, we walked Jyllian through the four questions.

"How do you think your mom would have approached a situation like this?" **(Question 1)**

"My mom was a single mom. Like I told you, my dad really wasn't in the picture after they divorced and he married the lady he cheated on my mom with. Everything was kind of on her, and I think it made her anxious. She felt a lot of pressure to get it right. She felt responsible for our family breaking up. She was always afraid that I'd get into something. She never really let me do much.

"So, were there ever any times you didn't want to tell your mom what you were up to? And how did she handle it?"

"Yeah. Honestly, I kind of hated telling her anything, because she'd always use it against me. She was so afraid of me screwing up my life that she micromanaged everything. I remember it got to the point that I would just not tell her things because I just needed some space. I know she loved me, but her constant anxiety was overwhelming. She made me feel suffocated."

"Did the fact that your mom responded that way make you want to draw closer to her or push you away?" **(Question 2)**

"I never really thought about it. We were close in a lot of ways. She went through so much. I know she was doing her best, but no. Now that you mention it, as much as I loved her, her constant nagging and worrying made me feel like she couldn't handle any extra stuff. I never really wanted to open up if I didn't have to. It would just add to her already full plate."

"So, you're saying that her approach didn't make it feel safe to draw closer to her?"

"I don't think I'd put it that way, exactly ... but, no. I know she wanted a closer relationship with me, but I was always afraid I'd break her. She was just so high strung about everything. I was a good kid. I really didn't get into much, but you'd never know it from the way she was constantly lecturing and nagging me. Even though I know she loved me, I didn't want to open up to her."

"Do you think you would want Meghan to feel like you couldn't handle whatever it was she needed to tell you? Do you think Meghan thinks that you're too fragile to handle the things she might be going through?" **(Question 3)**

Jyllian looked like the air went out of her. "I … wow. That's exactly how she comes across. Geez. That's awful. I would never want her to feel like that. Obviously, I'm concerned about her. I really do have a hard time trusting her. But I can see how maybe the way I'm going about things makes her feel like I did with my mom." Jyllian started to tear up. "That really sucks. I don't want that for her."

"I know you don't. I know how important it is for Meghan to trust you. How do you think that you could talk to Meghan about your concerns or the things that are going on in her life without making her feel like she has to take care of you instead of letting you disciple her?" **(Question 4)**

"Do you think that's how she feels? Gosh. I guess she does. This parenting stuff is hard. Honestly, I don't really know how to approach her. I guess instead of leading with all the lectures and horror stories about all the things I have going on inside my head, I could just talk to her? I'm going to need to think about that. One thing that's coming into focus for me is the fact that this isn't just about Meghan being a brat. I'm being too intrusive in the way I'm coming across. It's making her feel like I did with my mom. That's … really hard to think about. But maybe I just need to start by being honest about that and that I'd like a different relationship with her even if I'm not exactly sure how to do it."

Leading Jyllian through the four questions helped her see how she was accidentally pushing her daughter away even while she was trying to draw her closer. The insights she gained from this exercise helped change the conversation between her and Meghan. It allowed her to stop reacting to her daughter and start working with her daughter to rewrite the fearful script she was raised with.

The Four Questions Technique isn't a one-off exercise. It's meant to be an ongoing conversation that we have with ourselves. Get a notebook. Identify a parenting situation that is frustrating you. Write your answers to the four questions. Integrate this exercise into your prayer life. When you identify how you wish you could have felt toward your parents, ask your heavenly Father to help fill that void. Bring him the wounded parts of yourself and ask him to fill those dark spaces with his love. Then, look for ways to communicate that love to your teen. Let God heal you while you give your kids the gift of an even more grace-filled adolescence.

Inside Out Exercise

Another simple technique for dealing with the conflicted feelings that often accompany parenting is the Inside Out Exercise.

The Pixar film *Inside Out* tells the story of a little girl who struggles with adjusting to her family's move to a new home in a different part of the country. The film cleverly portrays the feelings of Joy, Sadness, Fear, Anger, and Disgust as distinct characters who live in her head. These five "people" have to learn to work together to help her navigate this difficult transition.

The film is actually based upon a psychological technique in which a person imagines their feeling as a separate person. For instance, you might describe your feeling of sadness as "a wrinkled, achy, tired old man." Or your anger as "a red-faced, tantrumming toddler." Or your resentment as "a sulky teenager dressed in black jeans and a T-shirt."

Researchers at the University of Texas conducted a study to examine the effectiveness of this technique. They had people describe an upsetting situation and rate their emotion on a scale of 1 to 10. Then they had the person describe their feeling as if it were a different person. What sort of person would the feeling look like? Once the participants anthropomorphized the feeling (i.e., described it as a person separate from them), the researchers asked the participants to rate the strength of their emotion once again. In every case, participants gave the feeling a significantly lower rating. They said they felt like the exercise helped them feel more detached from the negative feeling and claim more power over their emotions.[3]

For even greater effect, you can imagine having a conversation with this other "person." Specifically, imagine asking what that tired old man, tantrumming toddler, or sulky teen needs in order to feel loved and taken care of. You can even ask God to help you minister to this "person."

Although some people can feel a little silly doing this at first, it has an almost universally powerful and positive effect. Here are some examples of the exercise at work:

> *Eric, forty-four-year-old father of four children ages seventeen and under*
> When my kids get upset, I tend to take it really personally. Even if it has nothing to do with me, I get upset that they're upset. This "how dare you!" feeling just comes over me. My wife's told me I'm not comfortable with negative emotions. I'm not proud of it, but it's just the way I've always been. When I started using the Inside Out technique — I have no idea why, but the image that came to my mind … was of some lady in the Old South who, every time she encountered something that put her off, would get all huffy and say, "Whah ah NE-vuh!" and storm off. I'm not fond of that image. It's kind of emasculating, frankly. But I realized that wasn't an accident. When I get like that, I show my kids I'm not strong enough to listen and help them through their feelings. Anymore, when my kids start complaining about something, or start sharing how upset they are with the things going wrong in their life, I just imagine that high-strung south-ern belle having a histrionic moment. It reminds me that not everything is about me and that maybe what my kids need more than me being upset at them for being upset is a dad with strong shoulders they can lean on."

> *Elizabeth, thirty-eight-year-old mother of Gina, age fifteen*
> Gina can be really sarcastic. It's not disrespectful per se. It's not even necessarily directed at me. I just don't like it. I end up crit-icizing her for it, which makes her roll her eyes. Then I get hurt and start snapping at her about every little thing.
> I would like to help her be at least a little less sarcastic, but I realized that I needed to work on my approach. I imagined the part of me that gets so upset when Gina is sarcastic as a little girl on the playground who's sad because the Queen Bees won't let her hang out with them. I remind myself of that image when I

start to get my back up, and I tell that little girl that my daughter isn't rejecting her, and that she needs to let me handle it. It's funny, but I think doing that has let me do two things. First, I'm able to lighten up and laugh a bit more when it's appropriate. Second, when my daughter does cross the line, I'm able to correct her in a more gentle way. I notice that she's respecting my correction more now that I'm not responding to every sarcastic remark with the same level of irritation. It's really helped a lot.

Penny, thirty-eight-year-old mother of three children, ages sixteen and younger
I worry about spoiling my kids. They're actually really good. They're respectful. They help out around the house — even without being asked. They don't act spoiled at all.

The thing is, my family was really poor growing up. I was always the last of my friends to get the "new thing" if I got it at all, and then it was always the knockoff version. I never really minded so much, and I knew my parents always tried their best for me and sacrificed a lot, but my friends were merciless. My name is Penny, but the kids at school called me "Penny-less" growing up. I hated it.

My kids have never felt that, and I'm so grateful to God that I can give them more than I ever had, but when they ask me for things — even reasonable, nonmaterial things like going over to a friend's house — I have to fight through this resentful feeling. My first reaction is always to say, "No!" It's like there is this little girl inside of me that says, "No one ever gave ME anything. Why should I share it with you?"

My family really loves *Lord of the Rings*. The image that comes to mind when I think of that feeling is Sméagol, the Gollum who just wants the ring all to himself. When I get that feeling, I see Sméagol hovering over the thing my kids have asked for and hissing, "No! MY precious!" It actually makes me chuckle. Seeing that part of me in that light makes it easier for me to give my kids an honest, thoughtful yes or no instead of just turning everything into a power struggle from the outset. I don't always know exactly what to do, but at least it clarifies what I don't want to be like.

These techniques aren't meant to be a cure-all. If your strong negative feelings are consistently undermining your efforts to be the parent or person you want to be, it would be good to seek professional assistance to get some new tools. But for the typical, day-to-day resentment, anger, self-doubt, sadness, and irritability all parents occasionally face, this exercise can spell the difference between a positive interaction with your kids and a disastrous one.

Conclusion

Parenting can be tremendously difficult work. Besides the fact that parenting teens can be emotionally taxing, parenting also tends to bring up our own childhood wounds and the unresolved issues we have with our own families of origin. As Christians, we don't have to fear this reality. Instead, we should embrace it as the healing opportunity it's meant to be. God wants to break through all the noise and busyness of our everyday lives to remind us that even while we work hard to give as much love as we can to our children, God wants to give all of that love and more to the hurting parts of our hearts. After all, we are all his children, first and foremost.

Recommended Resources for Additional Healing

Parenting from the Inside Out: How a Deeper Self-Understanding Can Help You Raise Children Who Thrive (Daniel Siegel, TarcherPerigee)
Helps parents identify and address the emotional baggage that can steal the joy from parenting at every age and stage. A must-read for every parent, Siegel's book will be especially helpful to parents whose childhoods were less than ideal.

Homecoming: Reclaiming and Healing Your Inner Child (John Bradshaw, Bantam).
A classic self-help text, this book is particularly useful for parents because it walks readers through each developmental stage from infancy through adolescence, helping them identify both specific emotional

wounds and, more importantly, ways to heal the hurts within.

Unworried: A Life Without Anxiety (Dr. Greg Popcak, OSV)
Although this book offers a more general look at anxiety and anxiety disorders, the chapters on identifying and meeting needs (physical, emotional, spiritual, and relational), dealing with negative thoughts, and setting appropriate boundaries will be particularly helpful for parents — especially those who are anxious or self-critical about their abilities as a parent.

CatholicCounselors.com
Since 1999, our organization, the Pastoral Solutions Institute, has offered Catholic-integrated pastoral tele-counseling services for individuals, couples, and parents. If you need additional coaching/counseling services that respect your Catholic faith, we invite you to learn more about how we can help. Visit us at CatholicCounselors.com.

Prayer

Lord, help me embrace the priestly, prophetic, and royal dimensions of my parenting role so that I can heal the wounds that make it hard to love and be loved the way you want me to. Help me to consecrate every moment of my parenting life to you. Give me the grace to discover healthy, godly ways to meet my needs. Help me embrace your call to communion through loving service. Let me remember what it was like to be a teen — struggling to figure out how to navigate all the challenges. Help me give my kids the support I wish I had gotten. Fill me with your healing love so that I can give that same love to my kids. I give the broken parts of my heart to you. Make me whole in your love and grace.

Holy Family, pray for me. Amen.

Questions for Reflection

How does it change your perspective to think of Discipleship Parenting as a means by which God seeks to heal you as much as it is a way of raising godly teens?

In this chapter, we explored how parenting gives us the opportunity to develop the threefold mission of priest, prophet, and royal in baptism. How does this idea help you see the spiritual dimensions of parenting? How could this view help you connect more meaningfully with the ways God is trying to connect with you in your home — and specifically through your parenting role?

What personal needs are the hardest for you to meet on your own? How do you currently seek help meeting these needs? What more could you do to give yourself permission to identify your needs or seek help in meeting them in respectful ways?

Does the Four Questions Technique give you new insights into the aspects of parenting teens that are most challenging for you?

What emotions would you like to address by using the Inside Out Exercise? How does viewing these feelings as other people change your relationship with these emotions?

CHAPTER 10

Astray Like Sheep: Discipling the Misbehaving Teen

*Do not provoke your children to anger, but bring them
up with the training and instruction of the Lord.*

Ephesians 6:4

Although we often stray from the fold, Jesus, the Good Shepherd, is infinitely patient with us. As much as this gives us comfort, sometimes it's hard to be patient with *our* wandering sheep. Why do teens misbehave? How can we learn to respond as patiently as the Good Shepherd does with us?

Why Teens Misbehave: It's Not What You Think

Many people think that teens misbehave because they need to test their limits, to see how much they can get away with, or because they're manipulative or deceitful. This view sets up an unnecessarily adversarial relationship between parents and teens.

Protestant vs. Catholic View of Misbehavior

Sociologist Murray Strauss traced the notion that misbehavior, disrespect, and defiance are rooted in young people's negative (or even evil) intent to the Calvinist (i.e., Presbyterian) belief in the "total corruption" of the person. This is the idea that people are born bad and stay bad even after they encounter Christ, which is a foundational tenet of Calvinist theology. America is a nation founded by Protestants, and most Americans still unconsciously operate on Calvinist assumptions about why people do what they do. Many parents — even Catholic parents — simply inherit this bias from the culture. As Francis Cardinal George once explained, Catholics in America are "Catholic in piety but Calvinist in worldview."

By contrast, the Catholic understanding of the child is best summarized by Servant of God Father Edward Flanagan (founder of Boys and Girls Town), who said, "There are no bad [children]. There is only bad environment, bad training, bad example, bad thinking." Catholics recognize that sin certainly impacts us, but we do not believe that anyone is either born bad or born to *be* bad. Yes, we're born with original sin, but baptism washes away the stain of original sin, leaving us pure and clean through God's grace. Although it's true that, even after baptism, human beings still struggle to do the right thing, the Church tells us that this struggle itself (called "concupiscence") is not sinful (see CCC 405).

What does all this philosophy have to do with parenting? Everything. Sin disrupted the original attachment that existed between God, man, woman, and humankind before the Fall, but at our core, we are still good (see Gn 1:31). By working to rebuild healthy attachment, we help our kids tap into their natural, God-given desire to be good.

In general, the more securely attached our teens are, the harder they try to ask our counsel, listen to our advice, and work to please us. The opposite is also true. The more insecurely attached our teens are, the more they resist us and misbehave. Child development experts have a saying: "When children feel well, they behave well." This includes teenaged children. Recall the eight brain-based skills associated with secure attachment. Although teens get a bad reputation for being naturally narcissistic, research consistently demonstrates that healthy, happy, well-attached teens are naturally empathic, kind, attentive, and basically compliant.

Bad behavior is not a sign that your teen is bad. It's a sign that the teen is either hurting and needs help or that something is undermining the adolescent's God-given desire to see his or her parents as the mentors they are meant to be.

In light of these insights, instead of speaking of teens as "behaving" or "misbehaving," developmental psychologists now speak of kids as being either "regulated" or "dysregulated." These terms actually refer to the way teens' brains function when they're behaving properly versus when they're not.

Building the Well-Behaved Brain

Think of the brain as a house with a basement, a first floor, and a top floor. The basement is the cerebellum, the "body brain," which controls things like heart rate, respiration, and basic bodily functions. This is the most primitive level of the brain. The body brain is functional at birth, but it still needs some tuning up after birth to function at its best.

If we walk upstairs, the first floor of the mental house represents the limbic system, the "feeling brain," which is responsible for emotions, desires, and responding to threats. The famous "fight, flight, or freeze" response is generated here too. The feeling brain is largely in charge during the child's first three years of life, but it can be dominant in teens and adults as well. The degree to which a person of any age struggles to get past strong, emotional reactions is the degree to which that person tends to live in their limbic system rather than their "adult" or "thinking" brain.

Up the next flight of stairs, on the top floor, we find the cortex, the "thinking brain." This part of the brain is mostly undeveloped at birth and will continue to mature through young adulthood. In a sense, the cortex is framed out at birth, but construction will need to continue throughout childhood and well into young adulthood. The cortex houses all of our life experiences as well as the lessons we learn along the way. Ideally, these lessons enable us to manage our emotions well, meet our needs appropriately, solve problems effectively, and apply the rules to real-life situations in healthy and creative ways.

When a teen is well-regulated (behaving well), it means that these three parts of the brain are working well together. When this happens, in the face of a problem or stressor (e.g., hunger, sadness, fear, anger, excitement, confusion), the teen can accomplish three tasks:

1. Identify how that problem/stressor is affecting his or her body (body brain)
2. Identify the emotional reaction to that problem/stressor (feeling brain)
3. Use the information he or she has learned to put all of his or her physical and emotional energy behind the best response to the problem (thinking brain)

When a teen can do these three things, his mind is working properly. He can listen and behave.

By contrast, when an adolescent is dysregulated, he behaves poorly. This happens, basically, for one of two reasons. First, one of the three "floors" of the child's "brain house" might be sagging or collapsing. For instance:

1. The teen is hungry, tired, hormonal, or getting sick (body brain problem)
2. The teen is overwhelmed with feelings of sadness, anger, fear, or confusion (feeling brain problem)
3. The teen is confused about what to do in the first place — or how to apply what they already know — to a particular situation (thinking brain problem)

If any of these conditions exist, the dysregulated adolescent will behave badly because they can't figure out the best way to meet a pressing need. For instance, a young lady who is premenstrual and still learning how her period will affect her body may become moody or disrespectful. A young man who is experiencing an increase in testosterone as he develops secondary sex characteristics may become more impulsive and reactive. This represents a meltdown (dysregulation) in the body brain.

Similarly, a teen might melt down or lash out because he doesn't have the sophisticated emotional vocabulary he needs to deal with the pain associated with social rejection or those new, intense feelings of romantic longing (feeling brain dysregulation).

Likewise, a teen might know "the rules," but she might have a hard time knowing how to follow your rules in a manner that won't jeopardize her desire to maintain her increasingly important peer relationships (thinking brain dysregulation). In this last instance, even though a parent may feel as though "I've told you a thousand times ..." it can be hard for a young person's developing brain to connect the dots. They understand the consequences of disobeying the rules, but it may seem less costly than the fear of becoming a social pariah. Rather than simply punishing the teen in this situation, the wise parent will help the teen brainstorm ways to toe the line and still be able to maintain the good opinion of her friends.

Can You Hear Me Now? Can You ... Ugh ...

The second reason teens become dysregulated (i.e., behave badly) is that the "Wi-Fi" connecting the three floors of their brain house is buffering too much. There is a lot going on the average teen's brain, as new feelings, insights, and challenges come online. Sometimes, the three parts of the brain might be having a hard time communicating with each other.

For example, how often have you been grumpy or sullen because you physically felt "off," but couldn't put your finger on why (i.e., bad connection between body and thinking brain)? Or how often have you felt sad, angry, nervous, or frustrated, but couldn't imagine what you were so upset about (i.e., bad connection between feeling and thinking brain)? These experiences are caused by some kind of communication breakdown between the three parts of the brain. When we're regulated, the three parts of the brain are engaged in a metaphorical video chat, talking back and forth about what's happening in one another's lives and discussing how they might be able to work together to respond to it all effectively. But even if just one part's connection starts buffering, it prevents the whole brain from being able to figure out exactly what's going on or what the most effective response could be. Bad behavior results.

How often have you treated others poorly when you felt "off" or lashed out when your emotions got the better of you, even when you didn't know why? These are examples of times the different parts of your brain weren't communicating well. Think of how much harder it is for a teen who doesn't have your skills or life experience.

In light of these examples, it's easier to appreciate that your teen's bad behavior isn't caused by his desire to manipulate you, deceive you, or defy you. More likely, either one part of his brain (body, feeling, or thinking brain) is wrestling with a problem it doesn't know how to handle *or* the different parts of his brain are experiencing "connectivity problems" and, as a result, can't effectively coordinate their efforts.

This is especially true when your teen is in a situation that *feels* new (even if it isn't). To find solutions to new problems, we need to apply the information we've already been given in new and creative ways. That takes communication between the three brains. When your teen does something inappropriate, and you challenge them by saying, "Why did you do that?" they might stare at you blankly and say, "I don't know." They aren't lying. The panic they feel at being put on the spot makes their thinking brain shut down and their emotional brain take over. They *feel* shame, but they literally can't *think* well enough to explain why.

At this point, we'd like to take a moment to clarify a common point of confusion. When we use the term "dysregulated," we do not necessarily mean screaming, shouting, or melting down. The natural state for a well-regulated teen is respectful engagement and basic obedience. In other words, they may not always be ready to do what you say exactly when you say it, but they will at least try to respectfully address their concerns or questions and, assuming they feel heard, accept your decisions and guidance. This is normal and appropriate behavior to expect from a teen.

By contrast, a teen is dysregulated any time they're not behaving in the manner we described above. If you get anything less, there's most likely something that's at least slightly off in your child or in your relationship. You don't have to sound the alarm or call your therapist, but a sensitive and sincere, "You don't seem quite yourself today. You doin' okay?" is probably in order. As Benjamin Franklin put it, "A stitch in time saves nine." Most parents think that they have to wait until their child is so dysregulated that he or she is being openly defiant or losing it before they address it. This is not the case. If you feel ignored or get as much as an eye roll, you should use the techniques in the next chapter to make an appropriate mini-correction and help you and your kid get back on track.

Regardless, when your teen is dysregulated (i.e., behaving poorly) re-regulation (the return to appropriate behavior) occurs when you help your teen either address the unmet need that's at the root of the dysregulated response, or figure out how to help your teen handle the "new" (to him) situation. We'll talk about how to do this in the next chapter. For now, it's just important to understand what our Catholic faith and science have to teach us about where "bad behavior" really comes from so that you can be prepared to respond to it ... gracefully.

Attachment and Behavior

No matter how securely attached a person is, we all struggle with dysregulation to some degree. We cannot perfect ourselves via purely human efforts.

That said, research does consistently show that how securely attached a person is will predict their ability to avoid becoming dysregulated in the first place or more quickly re-regulate when they've been knocked off balance. There are two reasons secure attachment facilitates a person's capacity for regulation.

Reason #1: Brain Discipleship

First, recall the House of Discipleship we described in chapter 8.

When your now-teen went through toddlerhood and early childhood, you began discipling your child's feeling brain by doing things like:

- helping them find the words to express their needs and feelings appropriately
- giving your child extravagant affection so that they can learn to re-regulate by syncing up your more relaxed bodily rhythms to their own
- using gentle guidance and directed questions (not lectures) to help your child figure out the best way to respond to emotional situations
- creating household routines and family rituals that provide a safe structure to grow in

House of Discipleship

Stage Four: Relational Discipleship (Adolescence)

Teen turns toward parent to develop skills for having godly relationships and finding place in world.

Stage Three: Vocational Discipleship (Middle Childhood)

Child turns toward parent to discover and develop gifts in a way that helps him glorify God and make meaningful contributions to family and others.

Stage Two: Foundational Discipleship (Early Childhood)

Child turns toward parent to learn the stories, rules, and structures that lead to a love-filled, well-ordered life.

Stage One: Embodied Discipleship (Infancy and Toddlerhood)

Child turns toward parent to learn self-regulation and empathy through body-to-body communication.

By doing this, you taught your child's feeling brain that you are the person your child should turn to for guidance in managing his or her emotions.

In the preteen and teen years, you will focus more and more on discipling your child's thinking brain with practices such as:

- maintaining strong household routines and family rituals
- continuing to help your teens develop the vocabulary they need to express more and more complex emotions
- establishing ample one-on-one time to help your teens apply the lessons they've learned to increasingly complex personal and social challenges

At every step of the journey, the secure attachment fostered by Discipleship Parenting teaches the child how to identify and express their needs appropriately. Moreover, it establishes the parent as the child's go-to authority for meeting their physical, emotional, and cognitive needs in healthy, godly ways.

Reason #2: Building an Information Superhighway

The second way secure attachment facilitates good behavior is that it beefs up the "Wi-Fi" that connects the body brain, feeling brain, and thinking brain so that they can talk to one another more efficiently. By helping your teen learn to stay calm, giving her the vocabulary to express needs and feelings, and offering her clear ways to consistently meet her needs, research shows that parents foster the growth of neural connections between the body, feeling, and thinking brains. These cognitive "information superhighways" facilitate more rapid and creative communication between the different parts of the mind.[1] This helps teens respond more quickly and appropriately to various problems.

Making good moral decisions requires your child's brain to

- instantly apply the lesson they've previously learned to new situations;
- reflect simultaneously on what their feelings and needs tell them about that situation; and

- formulate a response that respects both of the above.

This process enables the teen to offer thoughtful obedience instead of merely slavish, dutiful responses (which are withdrawn when your back is turned). In order to pull this off, there need to be strong connections that facilitate near-instantaneous communication between the body, feeling, and thinking brains. You don't want your teen to have to think too hard and too long about the many moral decisions they face. If they do, they will become dysregulated and simply go along with the crowd instead of being able to think through a more mature response. Brain scans actually show how secure attachment creates these information superhighways. Our book *Beyond the Birds and the Bees* describes this process in more detail as it relates to raising sexually whole and holy kids.

Dropped Connections

Unfortunately, the more insecurely attached a teen is, the worse the "Wi-Fi" connection is between the different "floors" of the brain. For instance, anxiously attached people often struggle to hear their body brain at all. They don't do a good job of identifying when they need to sleep, eat, or otherwise take care of themselves. They don't tend to notice that they're falling apart … until they've fallen apart. They also exhibit spotty communication between the thinking and feeling brains. They may often feel anxious, insecure, and guilty, but have a very difficult time identifying why, much less knowing what to do about it.

Avoidantly attached people tend to be one giant thinking brain with very little communication between their feeling brain and body brain. They're dutiful, driven, and often successful, but their struggle to connect emotionally or see themselves as anything but "human doings" makes them ignorant of their feelings and susceptible to compulsive and addictive behaviors that numb their needs rather than meet them. Avoidantly attached people often lack insight. They attribute their problems, and even their emotions, almost exclusively to external factors because they struggle to have the internal dialogue that would allow them to understand what's going on inside them and how to fix it.

We share this to drive home two points. First, secure attachment is critical for helping the different parts of the brain communicate effectively so they can identify and meet their needs in moral and fulfilling ways. Second, parents with insecure attachment must do their best to address their own attachment wounds while they parent so that they can pass on healthy lessons in self-control, stress management, relationship skills, and problem-solving to their teens. Telling our kids isn't enough. We have to be able to disciple them.

The Church's assertion that parents are co-creators of life with God does not begin and end at conception. It continues through young adulthood. The secure attachment that parents cultivate with their children facilitates the brain growth and regulation that's necessary for good and moral behavior.

In sum, teens (and adults) behave badly when something is stopping the body brain, feeling brain, or thinking brain from functioning properly, or the connection between "floors" of the brain is spotty. When this happens, distraction, disrespect, and resistance result. By contrast, teens (and adults) behave well because their body brain, feeling brain, and thinking brain are each functioning well in their own right and communicating effectively with one another. When a person's whole brain is functioning well, the default response is attentiveness, rapport, and a genuine desire to do the right thing.

Working to maintain strong attachment with your teen helps you zero in on the factors that could be responsible for any dysregulation. Ultimately, this helps the adolescent stay regulated throughout the challenges of life.

Prayer

Lord, you have made me a co-creator of life with you not merely to have children, but to disciple them through every age and stage into a healthy, godly adulthood. Give me the grace I need to form my teen's mind so that their body, feelings, and thoughts can work together to glorify you.

Holy Family, pray for us. Amen.

Questions for Discussion

How does this understanding of the source of bad behavior challenge or confirm your own ideas about adolescent behavior?

Did it surprise you to learn that "dysregulation" refers to simple disobedience and not only to tantrumming, pouting, or meltdowns? What difference does this insight make to your understanding of what you ought to be able to expect from your teen and the quality of your relationship with your adolescent?

What difference would it have made if your parents (both your mother and father) had viewed your teenage misbehavior through the lens we propose in this chapter?

What healthy strategies do you use to re-regulate yourself when you become dysregulated?

What are some simple things you have done to successfully help your teen re-regulate when they've become dysregulated?

• • •

Conclusion to Part Two

Discipleship discipline represents a radical shift in the way we think about managing our kids' behavior. Instead of thinking of discipline as merely something we do to make kids behave and keep them out of our hair, discipleship discipline sees child-rearing as an ongoing relationship between a mentor (parent) and mentee (preteen/teen), who are learning from each other and growing together in grace.

Just as the Salesians (the order of priests and religious founded by Saint John Bosco) view their founder's preventive method not only as a system of child-rearing, but also as a key element of Salesian spirituality, discipleship discipline is an integral component of an authentic Catholic family spirituality. This approach not only helps you lead your child to God, but it also gives you a way to heal the wounds that might prevent you from rejoicing fully in God's love for you, conveying that love to your children, and growing in the virtues that enable you to become a whole, healed, grace-filled, and godly person.

Discipleship discipline invites us to remember that we are not raising our children in our image, but in God's. Likewise, it asks us to constantly reflect on how God may be speaking to us through the unique children he has given to us and how he might be asking us to grow through our relationship with them.

Seen through the light of discipleship discipline, parenting — and discipline in particular — isn't merely a nuisance we have to deal with so that we can finally get around to other, more profitable, spiritual practices. It is the primary way we encounter God's love, hear his voice, discover his will, discern his call to growth, and learn how he wishes us to minister to our closest neighbors, our children.

PART THREE

Filling Your Discipleship Discipline Toolbox

This system is all based on **reason, religion** *and* **loving-kindness.** *Because of this it excludes every violent punishment, and tries to do without even mild punishments. ... The practice of this system is all based on the words of St. Paul, who says: "Love is patient, love is kind, it bears all things ... hopes all things, endures all things." (1 Cor 13:4–7).*

Saint John Bosco on the Preventive System of Discipline

What most parents consider discipline techniques are, in reality, punishments. Discipline is different from punishment. As Saint John Bosco taught, godly discipline is primarily concerned with teaching a child what to do and providing the structure, support, and practice necessary for the child to succeed. By contrast, parents with a more worldly, punishment-oriented mindset believe that if they just make a teen suffer enough (by lecturing, yelling, or removing privileges), good behavior will spontaneously result. This punishment-oriented attitude represents the repressive system that Saint John Bosco decried. It's also a terrible way to learn anything.

When children get to about age ten, they are much less naturally inclined to do something because their mom and dad said so. This isn't defiance. It represents the fact that their brains have developed to the point that they need to understand why they are doing something — not because they want to challenge your authority, but because they need to learn how to apply the lessons you are trying to teach when you aren't there to tell them what to do. The more parents rely on punishment-oriented strategies to manage their teen's behavior, the more likely it is that they will raise a teen who ignores their rules as soon as the parents are out of sight. Believe it or not, this has less to do with defiance or willfulness than it does with being a kid who has never learned to think for him- or herself. This teen has been taught by Mom and Dad to simply go along with the most commanding presence in the room. The parent assumes — to their peril — that this will always be them. When they are not around, however, the teen will simply follow whatever other leader (adult or peer) steps into the void. Punishments teach nothing except blind obedience to whatever perceived authority (legitimate or not) happens to be in charge at this moment.[1]

Good behavior, even in adolescence, has to be taught. Because teens are all about relationships, the best way to teach your teen to do anything is by taking a more relational approach that models, encourages, teaches, and coaches instead of telling, shaming, lecturing, and punishing.

As we have asserted throughout this book, no matter how many tools you have in your toolbox, their effectiveness is directly related to the degree of attachment you have with your teen. A good rule of thumb is, "Rules without relationship lead to rebellion." You can't raise healthy, obedient teens — much less godly ones — if you rely on punishments to make up for a poor or nonexistent relationship with your child. If you take this approach, you will either burn out, give up, lower your standards (because they're too difficult to maintain), or find yourself engaging in a more and more adversarial relationship with your teen. Your efforts will simply cause your adolescent to become more sneaky, defiant, sullen, and rebellious.

That said, even parents who have an uncommonly good relationship with their children need good tools. The series of mini-chapters in this next section, Your Discipleship Discipline Toolbox, will give you a brief overview of our most common techniques, specifically the following:

Rituals and Routines
Collecting
Team-Building
Catch Them Being Good
Virtue-Prompting
Do-Overs
Rehearsing
Time-In
Emotional Temperature Taking
Time-Outs (Taking a Break)
Logical Consequences/Removing Privileges/Grounding

Part 4 will offer suggestions for applying these techniques in the various stages of your preteen and teen's development.

CHAPTER 11

Rituals and Routines

Although many parents think that it's normal for teens to not want to have anything to do with them, this is not true. Every adolescent's primary concern is either learning how to have rewarding relationships or practicing forming healthy relationships. Strong family rituals teach teens what healthy relationships look like. Family rituals help teens learn to set priorities, take time for reflection, make time to talk and share, and build real connection. The only time teens don't want to hang around Mom and Dad is when the lack of family rituals at home means "missing out on relating" or when an overriding adversarial relationship poisons family time. Assuming secure attachment and meaningful family rituals, teens can enjoy being home almost as much as they enjoy being with peers.

As you can see, rituals and routines are a critical part of discipleship discipline with teens. Without them, every other technique becomes harder to employ and bears less fruit. Second only to secure attachment, family rituals and routines are essential for raising well-socialized, emotionally (and even physically) healthy adolescents.

Rituals

The mission of Discipleship Parents is to raise kids who know how to live godly lives. By prioritizing daily opportunities to work, play, talk, and pray together as a family, Discipleship Parents model how Christians relate to work, leisure, relationship, and prayer.

Examples of daily family work rituals include things like:

- cleaning the kitchen together after meals
- picking up the family room together before bed
- folding laundry together
- cooking together
- doing light housework together

Examples of daily family play rituals include things like:

- playing cards or a board game together
- family reading-aloud time
- playing outdoor games and sports as a family
- doing family craft projects

Examples of daily family talk rituals include things like:

- meaningful family mealtimes
- family meetings
- discussing the highs and lows of the day
- discussing ways to make family members feel loved or cared for
- developing/reviewing a family mission statement

Examples of daily family prayer rituals include things like:

- grace before meals
- family praise and worship time
- P.R.A.I.S.E.
- blessing one another at the start of the day and before bed
- morning and bedtime family prayer
- attending Mass as a family
- family Rosary/chaplet

Daily, planned family rituals for working, playing, talking, and praying together are a catechism in Christian living. In our experience, the more a teen struggles to have good balance in his life, enjoy appropriate recreational outlets, engage in meaningful and appropriate conversations, and maintain a meaningful prayer life, the less likely it is that they experienced the corresponding rituals in their homes growing up. Family rituals for working, playing, talking, and praying together strengthen the heart of your home and form well-rounded, godly kids.

Rituals: Where Do You Start?

If you have not had strong rituals in your family up to this point, it isn't too late to start creating them. Start slowly, and work to get your kids' buy-in. In a family meeting, explain that you would like to be a better team. Give some practical examples of how you think being a better team would benefit your kids. For instance, you would all get along better. You (as the parent) would have an easier time getting to know their needs and how you could help. As a family, you would do a better job of making one another feel like you were there for one another. Ask how they think being more of a team might change the way your family relates.

Next, mention that teams don't just show up for game day. If they did, they'd step all over one another on the field. They have practices, meetings, fundraisers, and other activities that help them get to know one another in lots of different contexts. In a similar way, building a real family team means doing little things to work, play, talk, and pray together every day. As a family, generate a couple of things you could do — relatively easily — in each of these four categories.

Finally, talk about how you'll start doing these things. It's okay if you can't start all of them all at once. Be reasonable about integrating these activities into your already busy life. As time goes by, continue to have regular family meetings (a great "talk" ritual) to discuss how you're doing being a team and living out your rituals, and how you might need to change priorities or activities outside the family to have more time and energy to be the team you're working to become.

Routines

In addition to family rituals, which tend to involve more meaningful family interactions, strong family routines enable you to effectively manage the details of the day-to-day life of your home. They involve simple activities like:

- getting ready in the same way/at the same time every morning
- getting to bed in the same way/at the same time every evening
- welcoming children home from school in the same way every day
- handling meal prep and chores in the same way every week

At first, you might not think of these activities as an important part of parenting teens. It's true that morning and bedtime routines will change as kids get older, but no matter how old they get, people need routines to lead a healthy life. For instance, healthy adults don't just wake up when they feel like it, take as long as they want to get ready each morning (or get ready in a random order), and reinvent each day from scratch. They have a morning routine that helps them get out the door feeling put together and ready to take on the day. They wake up consistently at a certain time and get ready in a certain order. Ideally, they make a little time for prayer and reflection as well as a morning beverage and a light breakfast. Most of these morning routines will be largely unconscious, but they are nevertheless consistent. Maintaining them makes a huge difference, and disrupting or missing them can have a highly negative impact on the day.

Likewise, healthy adults don't just fall asleep wherever they happen to be when they get tired enough to pass out for the night. They have routines that enable them to go to bed in a manner that helps them get a good night's sleep. Perhaps they turn off screens for a time before they go to bed and take time to read a bit, pray a bit, make a plan for the next day, get into comfortable pajamas, etc.

Good routines are flexible enough to prevent life from being boring or regimented, while at the same time facilitating a sense of safety, order, security, and healthy predictability. Chances are, the degree to which these behaviors come naturally to adults is the degree to which they learned them growing up in a household that also valued routines.

Many parents think that putting teens in charge of their own time

— letting them choose when to get up, get to school, do chores, do homework, etc. — teaches independence. The opposite is actually true. When teens are left to "figure it out for themselves," they tend to take the path of least resistance and do nothing. The only time this isn't true is when a teen is raised in a household with strong routines for handling the activities of daily living that the teen has internalized over time.

Consistent family routines provide an environment where expectations are clear and good behavior can flourish. Strong household routines make it easier for kids to help with chores and be where they're supposed to be when they're supposed to be there, not because you had to tell them, but because "that's the way it is" in your house, and it simply never occurs to them to question it. Strong family routines create an orderly current that flows through the house and carries everyone along with it. Without strong routines, parents are stuck deciding on the fly when and how things should happen and then trying to force the kids to conform to their will. Over the years, strong family routines implicitly teach kids (i.e., without parents having to say much about it) that there is a place for everything and everything should be in its place (literally and metaphorically). It also teaches kids that when and how you do something matters, not just "getting it done when you feel like it." The key to raising teens to take responsibility for their own life and work without having to yell at them about it is to raise them in a home with solid routines that bring order to each day and create a rhythm for getting things done.

Routines: How Do You Start?

If you haven't had consistent routines in the past, use a similar approach to the one we described earlier in this chapter on building family rituals. Have a family meeting and talk about how you would like to have a less chaotic family life. Discuss practical examples of how having routines could benefit the kids. For instance, you might note that some weekday mornings (or any other part of the day) are much less stressful than others. Note that this is because you do certain things differently on those days. Get the family's help identifying those differences that have an impact. What time do you get up? How do you pace the morning? How do you create a little space to connect with God and/or one another? Finally, propose that you don't leave good mornings to chance. Suggest that you work together to take charge of creating a more positive start to each day by intentionally building these habits into a morning routine. Don't take no for an answer, but do discuss the kinds of routines that would actually work for your family. The discussion isn't about whether you should have routines, but how you can create workable ones.

Use a similar approach for chore routines and nighttime routines. When do things seem to spontaneously go better? What has helped you get through these activities feeling closer in the past? How could you be more intentional about creating routines that allowed you to replicate these successes? If you can't think of any times that have gone better in the past, discuss what your "ideal" experience of these times of day would look like. If you were going to do chores in a way that enabled your family to be a team and handle things in a more manageable, predictable manner, how would you all prefer to get them done? If you were going to create a nighttime routine that helped you feel connected to one another, and loved by one another, how would you do it? Would you straighten up the family room together before everyone went off to get ready for bed? Would you read aloud together for a bit? Take a little time for family prayer? With older teens, does their curfew need to allow them to participate in the family nighttime routines? What are the exceptions? (Note: There should always be some. Routines are helpful and flexible.) We can't give you a list of things you should or must do. Every family is different. But whatever habits they encompass, every family needs routines to function at their best.

Routines make up a kind of "rule of life" for families. Convents and monasteries don't just think of prayer when they think of their shared spiritual life. They also think of how they order their day. When and how they rise. When and how they gather and eat meals. How they get their work done together. All of these things create the peaceful atmosphere that allows their spirituality to flourish. Don't worry. The rule of life in your domestic church isn't meant to be monastic. Not at all! The routines that make up the rule of life in your domestic church shouldn't feel rigid or oppressive, but they should provide an implicit structure that allows your family to experience some sense of peace and order as you go through your day together. Routines create an orderly flow in your household that allows you the space to encounter Christ in the day-today activities of your life. When every day is up in the air, you don't have time to pray, or reflect, or listen to God. You're too busy reacting instead of living. Routines challenge this unfortunate condition that afflicts many modern households.

Creating strong family rituals and routines is as simple as it is countercultural. It starts by treating family time as the most important activity in the week and scheduling all other activities around it. Sometimes that means saying no to other extracurricular activities. That's okay. Extracurricular activities should always *enhance* domestic church life, not compete with it — even for teens. Some juggling between family rituals and extracurricular activities is always expected, but any activity that makes connecting as a family on a daily basis impossible *needs to go.* By all means, be supportive of your teen's need to develop outside interests and activities, but never be afraid to tell coaches, teachers, or even your parish ministers that your teen won't be able to attend a particular practice, game, or event if it conflicts too often with a family ritual or stretches your family routine to its breaking point. Prioritizing your family life is an important way that your domestic church can evangelize the culture.

Of course, it is critical to give teens the opportunity to be with their peers so that they can practice the relationship lessons you are teaching them. That can often require families to be as flexible as reasonably possible when it comes to negotiating the best way to maintain family rituals. Even so, there is no question that teens need regular family time. The best way to make sure they are getting the family time they need is to establish healthy rituals for working, playing, talking, and praying together, and maintaining those rituals throughout adolescence. Because family rituals are such an important part of an authentic family spiritual life, we discuss this topic at length in *Discovering God Together: The Catholic Guide to Raising Faithful Kids.*

CHAPTER 12

Collecting

I n order to get your teens to listen, you need to *collect* them first.
Imagine if a teacher walked into a junior high or high school class-room, picked up his briefcase, and as he walked back out of the room said over his shoulder, "Look kids, I have a ton of stuff to do today. I'll be back, but I need you to get all the problems on page 30 done. I'll check your work later" … then slammed the door and left. Would the assignment be completed? Would the teacher be justified in being upset when he came back and the majority of the students either failed to do the work or at least struggled to do it well? You would be lucky if the room was still in one piece!

It isn't unusual for parents to adopt a similar approach to discipline with adolescents. Walking through the living room, we see our kid in the middle of some activity and we say, "I need you to … (clean your room, take out the garbage, watch your sister, etc.)," and then we wander off to do something else. We return later only to become outraged that the thing we asked for didn't happen. We assume that since our preteens and teens look capable of following through, they should do just that.

Why is this an unreasonable expectation? Because we're no better. Imagine your spouse or kid walking through the room while you're do-ing something and saying, "Hey could you take care of thus and such for me?" Most likely, we'll barely look up and mindlessly say, "Um, sure." Then we'll promptly forget anyone ever asked us to do anything. When our kids do this, it is not usually because they are being disobedient. Mostly, it's that their attention is otherwise occupied, and they are simply not fully cluing in any more than we do when we're operating under similar circumstances.

Collecting helps avoid this predictable problem by making sure your teen is listening to you with their heart, not just their ears. It involves the following:

- Go to your teen (or *kindly* ask them to come to you).
- Engage them/Get their attention with affectionate contact (e.g., touch their shoulder, touch their hand, give them a hug).
- Communicate your expectation with a friendly tone ("Hey <Name>, what are you up to? Listen, I need you to …").
- Identify/resolve any problems that might stop the teen from successfully completing the task. ("I'll give you more time to do X later, but I need you to take care of this now." Or, "It's fine with me if you do what I asked as soon as you're done with your homework, but either way, it has to be done before you sit down for dinner."
- Ask them to repeat what they heard you say. ("Do you understand? Okay, good. Now, tell me what I just asked you to do.")
- Be sure you actually see them start to do what you have asked them to do, or have them come and tell you that they are going to start. ("Hey Dad, I finished my homework. I'm going to start on that thing you asked me about.") If you don't see them going off to do it, or if they don't tell you they are heading off to do it, you should assume it is not getting done. Follow-through is on you.
- Offer encouragement and let them know you're going to follow up.

Please note that these steps serve as a basic outline. The point of collecting isn't to follow a rigid template, but rather to walk through the basic steps that will allow you to help your teens become regulated enough to follow through with what you've asked.

Here is an example:

Liz sees her son, Francis (age fifteen), playing a video game in the family room. It's almost dinner time and she needs his help setting the table. She goes to him **(Step 1 — Go to teen)**, sits next to him, touches his arm **(Step 2 — Engage/Affectionate contact)**, and says, "I don't want to interrupt. Let me know when you can pause the game."

She waits about a minute, making appropriately supportive comments while he plays. If it starts to drag on more than a minute, she repeats her request more firmly, "I don't want to interrupt, but I need you to pause." Francis pauses the game.

"What's up?"

"There's about fifteen minutes to dinner, and I need you to start setting the table" **(Step 3 — Communicate expectation)**

"Ah, man. I'm almost done with the level!"

"So, I could give you five minutes to finish now, but that would be it. You'd have to stop even if you weren't at a save point. Or, if you pause your game now, I promise to give you fifteen minutes after dinner to finish up. Which would you prefer?" **(Step 4 — Identify and resolve obstacles)**

"Ugh. I guess I'll just come now."

"Okay, so what are you choosing to do?" **(Step 5 — Have the teen repeat expectation)**

"I'll come now. Can I have a little time after dinner to finish this level?"

"I just said you could."

"Cool."

Liz watches Francis save the game and they go to the kitchen together. **(Step 6 — Observe the teen complying)**

Liz says, "I know how much you love that game. It was really mature of you to be willing to take a break to help me. It really means a lot that I can count on you even when there's something else you'd rather be doing." **(Step 7 — Encouragement and promise to follow up)**

Your initial reaction might be, "That's great, but that takes a lot of thought and time." Honestly, though, if you re-read the exchange between Liz and Francis aloud — even allowing for the pauses — you'll see that it took about three to five minutes. That's a lot less time and energy than she would have spent if she just yelled from the kitchen, "Francis! Turn off the game and set the table!" only to end up fighting with him ten minutes later when she returned to find nothing done. Yelling from the kitchen — or asking Francis to set the table while she walked through the room — is "easier," but it almost always results in a frustrating outcome for the parent and the teen. It is just one way parents give away their power. Collecting allows you to see that your needs are given the attention they deserve.

CHAPTER 13

Team-Building

Teens are often accused of being narcissistic, but the fact is, we are all broken, sinful people. Learning to tune in and attend to the needs of others doesn't come naturally to any of us. Kindness, attentiveness, and self-giving are skills that need to be taught. If our child is narcissistic, we may have *told* them they should be more attentive to the needs of others, but we probably haven't actually given them the practical support they need to learn to actually do it. Telling isn't the same thing as teaching.

The fact is, teens are remarkably capable of bringing positive, practical ideas to conversations about solving common family and household problems, if we teach them how to do it. Moreover, teens like feeling that we respect and value their input. Parents of preteens and teens need to step out of the "it's up to me to tell them what to do" mindset and move into the "it's up to me to facilitate a conversation where all the family members work together to resolve problems and difficulties." The more we are able to communicate this respect, the more they tend to want to be part of the solutions.

Team-building is a technique that helps you tune in to others' needs. Team-building asks your whole family to consider how they can do a better job taking care of one another during a particular block of time (e.g., morning routine, time between coming home from school and dinner, time from dinner to bed).

Team-building has three steps:

1. Identify the time frame.
2. Ask how the family can take care of one another during that time period.
3. Create a concrete ritual to reinforce the change.

Here's an example:

Alicia, a working mom of three teen boys, Jim (seventeen), Max (fifteen), and Jacob (thirteen), was frustrated by how much of the housework tended to fall to her, especially once the school year was under way. Her husband and the kids would help out when asked, but most of the emotional labor involved in getting things done (identifying the task, making a plan to delegate or complete the task, following up to make sure it got done, etc.) fell to her. Things were especially bad after dinner, when everyone scattered to do their own thing, leaving her with the dinner dishes and whatever else needed to be done to keep up the house. She was burning out.

Having identified the time frame she wanted to work on, she called a family meeting.

Alicia said, "I know that we all have things to do after dinner, but a family is supposed to be a team. We're supposed to feel like we can count on one another and look out for one another. To be honest, I haven't felt much of that lately."

Alicia explained that she needed the family to be more intentional about working together between dinner and bedtime. She wanted everyone to have time to go to practices, do homework, and whatever else they needed to do, but she felt alone and needed to feel more like her family was a team.

Mark, Alicia's husband, helped Alicia list the various tasks that she needed more help with. Then he said, "You know, guys, being men, especially, means making sure the people we love feel taken care of by us. I know none of us have meant to, but we've really been letting Mom and one another down. How could we do a better job of working together to get these things done as a family?"

At first, the boys were a little resistant. They were concerned that working together to handle household chores more efficiently would mean that they would have to miss practices or spend all night getting work done. Mark and Alicia assured them that their activities were important, and that if they worked together a little bit every day, it shouldn't take much time to keep things up.

They decided that after dinner each night they would work together as a family, and then spend twenty more minutes doing at least one other chore together. They went over the list that Mark made at the beginning of the meeting and divided up the various chores throughout the week. Alicia wasn't sure whether everything could get done in that amount of time, and the boys were still a little worried that all the extra work would cut into their activities too much, but they agreed to give it a week and then renegotiate if any of them weren't happy. They also made a deal that as long as they could see each person really doing their best to get things done, then if they sometimes needed to leave early for a game or other scheduled activity, they would be excused. But if they hadn't been working hard, then they would have to stay until the work was done.

Each day that week, they spent a few minutes at the end of dinner reminding one another what work needed to be done. Once they finished with the dishes and cleaning up the kitchen, they did at least one chore — sometimes two — together. Because they were working together, they were surprised to see how much more quickly things got done. They also found themselves laughing together as they took the additional time to continue the conversations they started at dinner. It turned out that "chore time" wasn't just about getting things done. It actually helped them feel more connected too.

By the end of the week, everyone was convinced that the new work ritual was an improvement over the way they did things before.

Every family has certain times during the day (or during the week) when they find it more difficult to get along. Instead of accepting this as a necessary downside to family life, use the team-building exercise to make a plan for having one another's backs when you need it most. Identify a time frame in which you would like to get along or work better together, gather your team, and make a plan for how you will take care of one another in that specific time period. Instead of complaining about your teen's selfishness, teach them to be part of a team by asking, "How can we work together to be a better team so that (this time period) can go better moving forward?"

CHAPTER 14

Catch Them Being Good

Teens make a lot of mistakes. It's easy to fall into the bad habit of exclusively pointing out when teens fail to meet our expectations. A much better approach is to "catch them being good," noting good behavior with small gestures of affection and affirmation. Studies consistently show that simple, positive reinforcement produces consistently better outcomes than punishments and consequences.[1] Even teens want nothing more than to see the light of approval reflected in your eyes.

You don't have to throw a parade every time your teen does something that pleases you, but remarking on good behavior lets them know that you're actually paying attention *and* that you're glad to see them succeed. Here are some examples of catching teens being good:

"I really like the way you guys are listening to each other. I appreciate how respectful you're being!"

"It means so much to me when I see you starting your schoolwork without me having to remind you. I love how responsible you are."

"I know that you're frustrated, but I see how hard you're trying to be respectful anyway. That really means a lot to me. Thank you."

"I can see from the look on your face that your piano practice is really tough tonight. I really admire the way you're sticking with it. That's really impressive."

In each of the above examples, the parent remarked on a desirable behavior that occurred spontaneously and complimented the teen for the virtue he or she was displaying. Doing this also helps you deal with times when your kids aren't behaving well. How? Because they'll know exactly what you mean — from experience — when you ask them to show more responsibility, respect, or stick-to-itiveness. They'll know exactly what you want because you took the time to punctuate their successes.

CHAPTER 15

Virtue-Prompting

Teens are searching for their identities. It's up to us to help them identify and live out the virtues that will form the core of who they aspire to be as persons.

Although we don't recommend it, when kids are younger (under ten) parents can get away with "cheating" by simply telling kids what to do and making them do it "because I said so." When our kids are little, we're so much bigger than they are and they are so dependent upon us that they usually do what we ask without too much of a fuss. But as kids get older and move into the preteen and teen years, it becomes more and more important to help them think through what makes a good choice versus what constitutes a bad choice. Continuing to simply tell our kids what to do prevents them from learning to think for themselves. Despite our best intentions, it actually sets them up to unthinkingly defer to whatever "authority" takes our place in our absence — including the most dominant member of their friend group. Teaching your teen to "do what I say because I am in charge" is, ironically, the best way to teach your kid to give in to peer pressure.

Virtue-prompting is a simple exercise that teaches your teen to think morally without you having to resort to moralizing, lecturing, or punishing. Virtue-prompting involves asking leading questions to help your teen identify the virtues that can help them master a given situation.

Here are a few examples:

Annie (fifteen) is frustrated because her friends are getting to-gether after school, and she has homework. Despite trying to work with you to find another, reasonable time to get her work done, it looks like she is going to have to say no to her friends.

Mom says, "I know how frustrated you feel right now, but I also know how much you appreciate when your dad and I and your teachers compliment you for how responsible you are. In your heart of hearts, what do you really think is the most re-sponsible thing to do here?"

Annie frowns. For a minute she looks like she wants to fight, but Mom sees the awareness dawning in her eyes. "I guess I need to get my work done," she says, grudgingly.

"I think I'd have to agree with you," Mom says.

Annie blinks back her tears. "I know it's the right thing, but being responsible sucks sometimes."

Mom smiles understandingly. "It really does. I'm sorry, honey. But I have to tell you, I'm so proud of you for making the right choice even though it's hard. Tell you what, let's talk about what we can do to try to make this evening a little less awful."

By virtue-prompting, Annie's mom was able to avoid lecturing and, in-stead, adopt a supportive, nurturing posture. She was there to help her daughter make the right choice, support her through it, and then be there to help lighten the load when her daughter resolved to do the right thing even though it was hard.

Here is another example:

Bethany (sixteen-and-a-half) and LeAnn (fifteen) are arguing. LeAnn wants to wear Bethany's sweater. Bethany says that she doesn't want LeAnn to take it. She's afraid LeAnn will ruin it. Dad (bravely) walks into the middle of the drama.

"Girls! I get that you both love this sweater. It seems to me that, to resolve this, you're both going to have to be more gener-ous and considerate to each other. How could you approach this in a way that would show that you were really trying hard to be generous and considerate?"

Bethany pushes back, "But DAD, I love that sweater!"

Dad says, "I understand, and I'm not telling you that you have to give it to her. I'm asking you to both be as generous and considerate to each other as you know how to be. What would that look like?"

LeAnn steps up. "I mean, I know she really loves that sweater. Could I borrow your red jacket instead?"

Bethany sighs, "Yeah. But look. If you really want to borrow the sweater, you can. I just don't want it ruined. Will you be careful?"

LeAnn looks up. "I will."

Dad interrupts. "You girls are doing a great job, but I have to ask: LeAnn, if something happens to that sweater, what would you need to do to be responsible?"

LeAnn says, "I mean, I'd be willing to wash it."

Dad says, "But what if it fades or the stain doesn't come out? What would you have to do then?"

LeAnn looks tentative. "Buy a new one from my savings?"

Dad says, "I think that makes sense. That's a good idea. Is borrowing it worth the risk of having to buy a new one if something happens?"

LeAnn thinks hard. "Oh, never mind, I'll just wear my other outfit instead."

Dad says, "Are you sure? It's your choice."

LeAnn says, "Yeah, it's fine."

Bethany says, "Hey, would you like to wear those new shoes I got? They would go great with that blouse."

LeAnn says, "Really?"

Bethany answers, "Yeah, let's go see how it looks."

Dad says, "Good job, girls. I'm proud of you, LeAnn, for being so flexible, and that was really generous of you, Bethany. Thanks for sticking with it and working things out together."

In both of these instances, the parents didn't waste time trying to pressure, lecture, or punish their kids into doing the right thing. They set the *expectation* for good behavior and facilitated good emotional regulation by helping their teens see the big picture and remain solution-focused in the presence of their strong emotional reactions.

CHAPTER 16

Do-Overs

Do-overs are exactly what they sound like. They give your teen a chance to do things over *the right way*. This technique works best when your kid has either rushed through a task and done a poor job of it or disregarded your attempt to virtue-prompt. When using do-overs, be careful not to be antagonistic, and don't just settle for basic compliance. Focus on getting the right attitude as well as their best effort.

Here are some examples:

"You're so unfair!"

"I understand that you're upset, and I really do want to hear what you're trying to say. Can you think of a way to express your feelings to me respectfully?" (Virtue-prompt attempt.)

Teen rolls his eyes. In a semi-mocking, robotic voice, he says, "I feel upset, Mooooom. I am ve-ry sor-ry."

(Mom takes a breath. Reminds herself that this isn't defiance. It's dysregulation.) "I get that you're irritated about having to say it over, but I honestly want to hear what you're trying to tell me. Try again. I promise to listen if you can tell me respectfully."

Teen rolls his eyes again but uses a more civil tone. "I'm just really tired, and I don't want to have to clean my room."

"Thank you, that was better. But it's a lot easier to talk to someone who isn't rolling their eyes at me. Take a breath and try one more time. I promise I'll listen if you approach me like I'm an actual person instead of your enemy."

Teen takes a breath. Uses a reasonable tone. "Mom, I'm really wiped out from baseball practice. Could I clean my room some other time?"

"I really appreciate you asking me so respectfully."

In this instance, having gotten the child to re-regulate and approach you more respectfully, you could either choose to let him suggest another time to clean his room if you were actually 100 percent sure it would get done then, or you could gently insist that it be done then anyway. For instance:

> "I really appreciate you asking me so respectfully, and I would normally be open to your suggestion, but we have to go out after dinner, and you won't have time to do it tomorrow. I know it's hard to do chores when you're tired, but thanks for being willing to do it anyway."

Again, notice that Mom retains her power by assuming that cleaning the room is a foregone conclusion. She doesn't ask whether it's okay if her teen cleans his room. She thanks him for doing it, even though it's hard.

Here is another example:

> You've asked your daughter to fold and put away her clothes. She acknowledges your request, and you see her take the laundry basket to her room. Later, you notice that her clothes are all stuffed in the drawers in a haphazard way. Some of them are hanging out of the drawers. You call her.
>
> "Honey, could you come here a second?"
>
> "What, Dad?"
>
> "I was really grateful when you said you would put your clothes away, but do you really think you gave the job your best effort?"
>
> "But I put them away!"

"I know. I'm asking if you really gave your best effort to what I asked you to do."

"Um … yesssss?"

(Dad says nothing. He just keeps looking at her.)

"Um … no?"

"Thank you for being honest. I agree. We both know you can do a lot better. Look, I'm going to need you to do this over. Please take everything out of your drawers, fold it properly, and put it away like you promised you would do in the first place. Do you understand?"

Her face is turning red and her eyes are watery. "Fine."

"Come here, Hon." Dad gives her a hug. "I know you're frustrated. Everybody is tempted to cut corners now and then, but I'm proud of you for being willing to do it right this time. I love you. I'll be back to check on you in half an hour."

Again, the father in this example was firm. He was clear about his expectations, and he didn't give away his authority by trying to argue with his daughter. He made it clear that he expected her best effort. Rather than lecturing her that she'd better do it right the next time or, worse, leave the clothes as they were but apply some unrelated punishment, he *expected* that she would do it right *this time*. He didn't try to talk her out of crying. He didn't react or call her manipulative. He recognized that was just a symptom of the dysregulation. He was affectionate, firm, and showed that he was invested in her success by promising to come back and check on her progress in a reasonable amount of time.

Do-overs are not punishments. They are, however, good discipline. They're meant to be an opportunity for the child to do what you asked, do it right, and see that you can be pleased when they genuinely give you their best effort.

CHAPTER 17

Reviewing

Reviewing enables you to help your teen anticipate and head off potential problems. Younger children tend to need more physical rehearsal. Because preteen and teen brains are better developed, they don't necessarily need to physically rehearse doing the right thing, but it can still be helpful to give them an opportunity to think through situations ahead of time, so they can be prepared to respond to the challenges they might face.

Whether your teen has never encountered a particular situation before or they have performed poorly in a specific situation in the past, make sure to help them review what a better response would look like before allowing them to walk into that situation again. The steps of reviewing are as follows:

1. Understand what the concern is
2. Identify the goal
3. Identify possible solutions
4. Solve for complications

Here is an example:

Carla is the mom of Luke (age seventeen). He is active in sports and plays soccer for his high school. Last week, Luke attended a party that one of his teammates was hosting. His teammate's parents were supposed to be there, but they left at some point, and some of the kids started drinking. Luke ended up joining in. He didn't get drunk, but Carla smelled alcohol on his breath when he came home. She grounded him for two weeks and suspended his driving privileges, but she knew that this, alone, wasn't enough to really address the problem. The next day, when she had cooled down, she knocked on his door. She sat down on the bed — where he was moping — and gently rested her hand on his shoulder.

"I would really just like to understand why you decided to drink at the party. You're usually so responsible. Can you help me understand why you had such a hard time being a responsible person this time?"

"I don't know."

"I get that you're frustrated. Why don't you start by telling me how it all went down? When did everyone start drinking, and how did you end up joining in?"

Luke sighed. He explained that when Kyle's parents left the party, Kyle started passing out beers. He said he wanted to toast the team's victory against their main rival last week. Before he knew it, Kyle shoved a beer in Luke's hand. Everyone popped open their cans and took a swig. He didn't know what else to do. He said he pretty much just nursed the one beer the rest of the night. He didn't really even like the taste, but once everyone else started drinking, they just assumed everyone would want to. He felt weird making a scene.

Carla responded, "That must have been really awkward for you. Obviously, I wish you had made better choices, but I think I understand how it happened."

Luke seemed relieved. "Thanks, Mom. I thought you'd freak out."

"I mean, I'm not happy. But what's the point of shouting at you or lecturing? You already know I don't approve. Honestly, I'm more interested in helping you figure out what to do in the future."

"I guess I just won't drink."

"Well, I appreciate you saying that, but I think it's harder than that, or you wouldn't have been drinking the last time, right? Just imagine that you're at some other party in the future and someone puts you in a similar position. What do you think you would do if you had it to do over again?"

"I don't know. I guess just say, 'No thanks?'"

"Look, can you just be a little more honest with yourself and with me? While I appreciate you saying that, what do you think would happen if you made it an issue with Kyle that you didn't want a beer?"

"He'd probably ask why I didn't want to toast the team and make a big deal out of it."

"Right. And then what would happen?"

"Same thing, I guess."

"Right. Thank you for being straight with me. And would I want you to be able to stand up for what's responsible if it came down to that? Of course I would. But can you think of anything else you could do to handle the situation without having to turn it into a big deal?"

"I guess I could have just taken the beer, but then put it down and gone and gotten a soda. As long as I had a can in my hand, I don't think anyone else would notice or care, really."

"That's a good idea. I like the way you're thinking through this. But what if there wasn't time? Like, what if they handed you a beer and just went into the toast?"

"I guess I could just raise the can and pretend I was going to take a drink but then go get a soda."

"Do you think that would work?"

"Yeah. I think so."

"Great. I'm glad we could talk that out. But listen, there's one more thing. You should never have been put in that position in the first place. You were literally set up to fail, and I'm not as upset with you as I am with the situation. Kyle's parents promised me that they'd be there. They never should have left you guys. I know you're almost seniors, but legally, his parents are still responsible for anything that goes on in their house. If someone had gotten trashed and gotten into a car accident, they could have been held responsible, and in some cases — like if someone died — they could even go to jail. I don't want you to be in that situation again if we can help it. If you're ever at a party and the responsible adults aren't there, how do you think you would handle it in the future?"

"I guess I could text you."

"Yeah. I really need to know if that happens again. I need to know that I can trust you to be responsible enough to let me know if that's going on. If that happens — even if nothing bad is happening — I need you to let me know. We can come up with some reasonable excuse why you have to leave, but I need to be able to trust you to not let other people put you in a position where you are being set up to fail, or I can't let you go in the first place. You get that?"

"Yeah, I do."

"Great, so tell me again how you're going to handle situations like this in the future."

"If the parents aren't there, I'll text you right away so we can figure out how to handle it. And if somehow someone gets me a beer or something anyway, I don't have to make a big thing about it, but I should just put down the beer and grab something else to drink as soon as I can."

"Great, and if someone asks you about it?"

"I'll just tell them I want to finish whatever I'm drinking first. They'll probably forget by then anyway."

Carla said, "Well, look, I expect to keep talking about this with you, but I appreciate you being willing to work this out with me. I just want to help you and make sure you don't ever feel like you're being put in an awkward situation you shouldn't have to deal with."

"Thanks, Mom. So, like, does this mean I'm not grounded?"

"Um, no. But nice try. It just means that I think I'm raising a young man I can actually learn to trust again instead of having to make you my prisoner for the next fifty years. So, can I trust you to do this once you're off grounding?"

"Yeah. I promise."

We want to be clear: Underage drinking is a very serious offense. The point of this dialogue was not to present a one-size-fits-all response to this particular issue. If Luke had been less agreeable, Carla might have had to take a much more directive approach, or even seek professional help. That said, the point of this was to show that the reviewing technique can work with even the most serious situations. Any time your teen is about to go into a situation they've never had to handle before, or when they have handled something poorly, use the reviewing technique to increase their chances of future success by following these steps:

1. Understand what the concern is
2. Identify the goal
3. Identify possible solutions
4. Solve for complications

CHAPTER 18

Time-In

We'll talk about time-outs and grounding shortly, but long before you get to the point where you need to use time-outs or grounding, time-ins are a much more effective way to help your teens re-regulate.

Remember, poor behavior is caused by dysregulation. Dysregulation occurs when a child is struggling to meet their needs, apply their skills, or manage their emotional temperature. Teens, in particular, can become dysregulated when they feel disconnected from their parents.

Research by the Gottman Institute found that defensiveness increases between two people when the ratio of positive to negative interactions between them drops below 20:1.[1] That means that if we want to increase the likelihood that our teens will respond positively to us, we need to make sure we are twenty times more friendly, encouraging, affectionate, affirming, kind, and thoughtful than we are criticizing, nagging, correcting, lecturing, or disapproving. As this ratio decreases, defensiveness increases.

If simple correction of your teens isn't working; if your attempts to guide your teens are being met with resistance or irritation; or especially if your teen is habitually doing things to irritate you despite you having corrected them numerous times … don't escalate to harsher punishments. Instead, get some time-in.

Time-in is similar to collecting in that it relies on increasing your teen's connection with you to help them get their emotions back under control. The difference is that while collecting happens *before* your teen seems stressed or upset, time-ins happen when you notice that your teens seems "off." Time-in consists of affectionate, one-on-one time with your kids that helps them re-engage the "calm-down system" in their brain (the parasympathetic nervous system).

Imagine that, for whatever reason, your relationship with your teen seems a little strained. Not necessarily horrible — just not quite right. You might notice a little more attitude than usual. Perhaps your teen has been a little more disrespectful than usual. Maybe they've been a little more resistant to your input, guidance, or requests for help. This sense of resistance you are getting from your teen is almost always a sign that you could benefit from some time-in, in addition to whatever consequences or strategies you might use to keep basic order. In this case, time-in might involve special one-on-one time doing a project together, going for breakfast or dessert, or engaging in some other enjoyable, interactive activity (i.e., not watching TV or going to a movie) that helps you get back in sync with each other.

Let's say that you've needed to correct your teen more than usual in a given week. Thinking about it, you realize that you haven't gotten a lot of one-on-one time lately. You continue to put out the little fires as they come up, but you also start planning to get some time together. You invite your teen to go to breakfast on Saturday. During breakfast, you focus on making the time as pleasant as possible. You let your child lead the conversation. You show genuine interest in what they're saying. You ask questions. You let them teach you about their life and interests. About three-quarters of the way through your time together, you mention that you've noticed that things have seemed a little "off" between the two of you lately. Without going into lecture mode, you mention a few examples just to illustrate what you mean.

Next, you ask whether something has been bothering your teen. You mention that sometimes people have a hard time being cooperative when they feel frustrated about something, but they don't know what to do about it or how to even talk about it. You ask whether there is anything that they need to talk through, and you listen patiently as they explain any concerns.

Using the team-building strategy we outlined earlier, you identify ways to work together better in those situations the next time they come up. Once that's done, you thank your child for being willing to work through this and tell them how proud you are of them for being so grown-up. You spend the last few minutes of your time-in talking about something more pleasant so you can end on a good note.

The time-in strategy allows you to intentionally make a deposit in your child's emotional bank account so that, when you ask for their obedience, they don't respond as if you're overdrawn.

Some parents react negatively to time-in. They feel as if they're being asked to reward their child's bad behavior. This attitude is based on the assumption that kids are naturally inclined to do bad things and be annoying. Remember, neuroscience tells us that the *normal state* of well-attached, well-regulated teens is compliance — even cheerful compliance. If a teen is having consistent problems behaving well, that means something is threatening the attachment between the parent and teen, or the teen is struggling to deal with something that's making him feel overwhelmed. Time-ins address both of these concerns by strengthening your attachment and allowing you to help your teen to address whatever might be upsetting them. By doing this, you reinforce your discipleship relationship by sending the message, "There is nothing I am unwilling to help you through — even problems with me." Communicating this via consistent use of time-ins is much more effective than simply saying, "You can tell me anything," and then wondering why your child doesn't.

CHAPTER 19

Emotional Temperature-Taking

There are fewer more stressful times in life than adolescence. Between the hormones and the more complicated social issues to negotiate, the teenage years are fraught with situations that are bound to raise any teen's emotional temperature — never mind yours!

As we mentioned earlier, an elevated emotional temperature leads to chemical changes in our bloodstream that literally shut down our ability to reason and think. The higher our emotional temperature, the more reactive we become. The emotional temperature-taking technique gives both you and your children a way to consciously recognize when they are in danger of becoming dysregulated. Once you've got the basic idea, the technique is almost infinitely adaptable.

Imagine a scale that goes from 1 to 10, with 1 representing *completely calm and regulated* and 10 representing *completely dysregulated*. A 6 represents the times we discussed in the last chapter when a person (you or your teen) just feels "off," even though, outwardly, things seem fine.

The scale is not based on your own or your teen's impression of how they feel. It's based on how they're behaving. Also, please note, a higher emotional temperature does not mean that your teen is necessarily being hostile or melting down. Some kids get quiet and withdrawn. Use

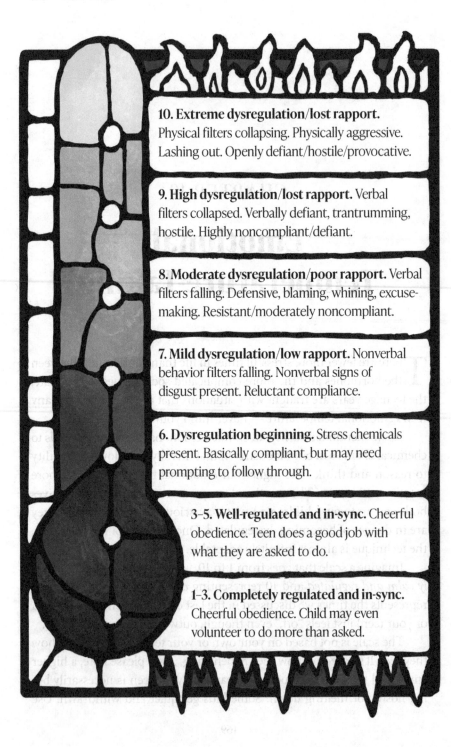

10. Extreme dysregulation/lost rapport. Physical filters collapsing. Physically aggressive. Lashing out. Openly defiant/hostile/provocative.

9. High dysregulation/lost rapport. Verbal filters collapsed. Verbally defiant, trantrumming, hostile. Highly noncompliant/defiant.

8. Moderate dysregulation/poor rapport. Verbal filters falling. Defensive, blaming, whining, excuse-making. Resistant/moderately noncompliant.

7. Mild dysregulation/low rapport. Nonverbal behavior filters falling. Nonverbal signs of disgust present. Reluctant compliance.

6. Dysregulation beginning. Stress chemicals present. Basically compliant, but may need prompting to follow through.

3–5. Well-regulated and in-sync. Cheerful obedience. Teen does a good job with what they are asked to do.

1–3. Completely regulated and in-sync. Cheerful obedience. Child may even volunteer to do more than asked.

the following behavioral symptoms to gauge your child's place on the emotional temperature scale. You might also find yourself in these descriptions.

From 1 to 3 on the emotional temperature scale ...

Your teen is completely in sync with you and almost perfectly well-regulated. At this level, they're affectionate, unusually empathetic, and capable of both cheerful obedience and willingly going above and beyond what you have asked them to do. You shouldn't expect your teen to be in this range all of the time, but it should at least be a semi-regular occurrence in a well-attached household with good rituals and routines.

From 3 to 5 on the emotional temperature scale ...

You and your teen are in sync with each other and your teen is very well-regulated. At this range your teen is capable of doing what you ask with a good attitude; although, as you get closer to 5, your teen might need a little extra prompting to prevent them from getting distracted and to follow through as well as they should.

At 6 on the temperature scale ...

Your teen is able to be compliant, but it's obvious that it's requiring a little more effort for them to do so. At this temperature, your teen may seem a little distracted, tired, or frustrated. This is because stress chemicals like cortisol and/or adrenaline are beginning to drip into their bloodstream. At this level, your teen will respond to you, but you might have to ask more than once to get their attention. Things just seem "off." This would be a good time to use some basic collecting and time-in techniques to help your child reconnect with you and re-regulate himself or herself before sending your child off to do whatever you asked. At this temperature, collecting is more of a preventive tactic and shouldn't take more than a minute, but the investment is time well spent.

At a 7 on the emotional temperature scale ...

Stress chemicals are building up in your teen's brain and bloodstream, shutting down the nonverbal behavior filters in their brain. A teen at a 6 or lower doesn't roll their eyes, huff and puff, fidget, grimace, or have a hard time looking at you when you're talking to them. At a 7, however, the brain-based self-control mechanisms that would normally prevent these behaviors are going offline. At this temperature, your child will have a hard time not showing outward signs of disgust, irritation, or frustration about almost anything. If you see these behaviors, don't take them personally. They have nothing to do with you. Your teen is effectively being poisoned by his own brain chemistry. He may be tired, hungry, frustrated, or otherwise wound up for some unknown reason. That doesn't justify disobedience, but it's a reason to pause, collect your child, and/or give him or her some time-in.

At a 6, collecting and time-in were preventive. At a 7, you will use those techniques to reset your child, as they are beginning to go off track. If you become heated yourself, you will most likely trigger a major disruption. Instead of giving away your power by fighting your teen, hold on to it by offering up a quick prayer, controlling your own reactions, and helping your teen re-regulate. Use collecting and/or time-in to get your child back down to a 5 before sending your child to do what you need them to do. It may take two or three minutes at this stage, but it's worth the effort. That might not seem like a lot of time, but if you address the tension this early in the game, it's plenty. The higher you allow your emotional temperatures to get, the longer it takes to reset. If you find that it consistently takes longer than two or three minutes to reset yourself or your teen, you may be underestimating how high your emotional temperature actually is. If that's the case, consider using the suggestions in this chapter a notch or two earlier until it begins to come naturally to you.

At an 8 on the emotional temperature scale ...

At this level, your teen is strongly "under the influence" of the stress chemicals in their bloodstream. Your child's nonverbal filters have now collapsed. Their verbal filters are under attack. Your teen may not be yelling, screaming, or openly defiant, but they will be whiny, defensive, blaming, begging, and saying things like, "Do I haaaaave tooo?" and "It's not FAAAIIIRR!" Some teens may start tearing up or become very quiet, sullen, and unresponsive. Again, it's never a question that your teen needs to do whatever you ask him or her to do. But if you see your child behaving this way, collecting and/or basic time-in will be critical. In adolescence, plan on this taking at least ten to fifteen minutes, possibly longer. That may feel inconvenient, but if you try to push your teen past this point without collecting him or her first, you will most likely provoke a major conflict that will exhaust both of you.

At a 9 on the emotional temperature scale ...

Your teen's verbal filters have fallen. They're officially melting down and/or being openly disrespectful and defiant. Alternatively, some teens will just shut down, turn in on themselves, become sullen, and withdraw. They may not say anything mean, but they won't do what you asked and they won't answer your questions. They will just stare at you.

At a 10 on the emotional temperature scale ...

At this level, your teen is officially out of control. Their nonverbal, verbal, and physical filters have collapsed. They're now hitting, throwing, or fighting with you on top of everything else.

Please note, as deeply offensive, unacceptable, and intolerable as these behaviors truly are, it is not helpful to simply write them off as "defiant." To do so sets up a fear dynamic, where the parent believes that his or her power is actually being threatened. Don't give your power away by assuming for one minute that you could be overthrown. Instead, do your best to view these behaviors as signs of a high level of dysregulation. Your child is being poisoned by their own stress chemicals. In such situations, your job as the parent is not to battle for control with your teen, but rather to assume control of the situation by consistently intervening to help get your child back into a state of self-regulation. Ideally, you will do this long before your teen gets to a 9 or 10 on the emotional temperature scale, but even if you don't, your job is the same. Resist the temptation to battle for control. As the parent, *you are* in control. Contain the situation. Empathize with the pain. Redirect toward solutions.

Every teen gets to a 9 or 10 occasionally, but if your child constantly seems to be at a 9 or 10, you will either need to clue in much sooner to your teen's emotional temperature, learn to do a much better job managing your own emotional temperature (because you can't teach your child what you don't practice yourself), or you may need to seek professional help for yourself or you and your teen together.

In addition to using this temperature chart to know when and how to intervene, we recommend teaching your child to identify their emotional temperature and helping them learn to ask you for help, or some time-in, or assistance finding a calming activity to do when they need to re-regulate. Teach your teens to use the chart in this book. Have regular conversations about their emotional temperature (again, based not on feelings but on the objective behavioral signs), your emotional temperature, the temperature of your household, and what you can do to help keep the emotional temperature lower for everyone. Learning to self-regulate is a critical lesson that should be learned and mastered in early and middle childhood, but if your teen is lagging in this area, now is the time to focus your efforts.

One last note on the emotional temperature scale. Some parents indicate that their children go from "a zero to a 10." This is not actually the case. Teens who exhibit this tendency to rapidly escalate are most likely operating at a 7 or 8 all the time without you realizing it. They escalate quickly because they are always just shy of exploding, and they don't have the emotional bandwidth to handle any additional stressors. If this describes your teen, begin looking at the bigger picture for what might be causing your child to live at such a high stress level. Do your best to identify and address those issues to lower the baseline emotional temperature. If you are unsuccessful identifying or resolving these problems, seek professional help.

CHAPTER 20

Time-Outs (Taking a Break)

Sending a teen or preteen to their room as a punishment is both silly and ineffective, but that doesn't mean there isn't a place for time-outs even for adolescents. That said, there are a few things you need to know about time-outs to make them work with teens.

A proper time-out is never meant to be used as a punishment. It's meant to give the teen and the parent some time to calm down so that they can re-engage a problem-solving conversation in a more solution-focused manner.

Time-outs should never be your go-to, first-line strategy. They should only be used when your teen is at an 8 or higher on the emotional temperature scale, and then *only* if your attempts to respectfully communicate and problem-solve together are in danger of breaking down. With teens, time-outs should be treated not so much as a punishment, but as an opportunity to "take a break." It is how we teach our children to step back in the middle of a disagreement, reflect on our approach, and cultivate empathy for the other person's position so that we can re-engage in the conversation in a more productive way. In fact, with teens, we prefer the term "taking a break" to time-out, as it more accurately reflects the intention of the intervention. Here are the steps to effectively take a break when in conflict with your teen:

1. Attempt to collect/redirect the teen. Follow the steps out-

lined previously in this book.

2. If this fails, insist that you and your teen need a break. The point is to separate and spend some time reflecting on what each of you needs, how to work together to meet those mutual needs, and also take responsibility for any offenses or disrespect that might have been committed in the earlier attempt to solve the problem.

3. Debrief
    - Discuss: "Where are we at?"
    - Sincere apology (to each other, if necessary)
    - Identify alternative behaviors/Outline way forward
    - Re-engage in problem-solving conversation

4. If your teen is too upset to successfully complete any or all of the above, repeat these steps as necessary.

Let's walk through this together.

1. Attempt to collect/redirect the teen

Before asking your teen to take a break, try to help them re-regulate in regular conversation. Say something like, "I love you and I'd like to work through this together. I get that we disagree, but I'm not your enemy. Let's listen to each other and work together to figure this out."

There is a chance — especially if the teen has already escalated to somewhere between an 8 and a 10 on the emotional temperature scale — that your attempts to help them calm down will actually inflame the situation. They're dysregulated and reactive. The equivalent is when you're upset and someone tries to give you a hug, only to have you say, "DON'T TOUCH ME!" Teens get to this place much more easily. If your teen is at this place, say, "I am trying to work through this together, but if you aren't ready to do that, you can go to your room and we can take a break until you're ready to pick this up again in a more productive way. How would you like to handle this?" Give them an honest choice between getting your help and giving them the space to work through things by taking a break first.

Again, taking a break is not meant to be a punishment (even if your teen acts like it is). It's an opportunity to give the teen a quiet place to get himself back down to at least a 6 so that you can re-engage the situation in a more solution-focused, respectful manner.

2. Take a Break

It's good to make this process as natural as possible. If collecting/redirecting fails and it becomes necessary to take a break, simply say something like, "I know we can get through this, and I'm committed to really listening and working with you, but I need to know that you can do the same for me. Go to your room for a bit. I'll come by in about ten to fifteen minutes, and we'll try again. While you're in there, think about what you want to say to me and how to say it respectfully, *and* try to come up with some ways to address your concerns that take my concerns into account. I promise to do the same."

Taking time apart does little to facilitate problem-solving on its own. If two people spend time apart but don't try to build some degree of empathy for the other's position while they are taking a break, they will simply pick up where they left off, and give all their energy to trying to prove how the other person is wrong. By telling your teen that the goal of taking time apart is having them identify solutions that also take your concerns into account, you are teaching them that the goal in a disagreement is not trying to pile up arguments to prove the other person wrong, but to listen to each other and identify solutions that take each other's concerns into account.

3. Debrief

- Discuss: "Where are we at?"
- Sincere apology (to each other, if necessary)
- Identify alternative behaviors/Outline way forward
- Re-engage problem-solving conversation

When you go to your teen, first check and see how they are. Are they re-regulated enough? Is their thinking brain back online? You'll know this by their facial expression and tone when you enter the room. If they are still upset, gently say, "I love you and I want to work this out, but I see you still need some time. I'll check back in a bit. In the meantime, please think about some ways to handle this that respect your needs but also take my concerns into account. I'll be back."

Assuming your child's emotional temperature is lower (based on their behavior toward you) and their thinking brain is back online, take a moment to assess where things stand. Say something like, "I'd like to talk through this together. Are you in an okay place to do that?"

If your teen is ready to talk, start by clearing the slate. If you need to apologize for anything you said or did, lead the way. Be the example of the humility you want to see in your teen. "Listen, I was frustrated that you were speaking to me in that really disrespectful tone, but I'm sorry I yelled at you. I love you. Please forgive me."

If your child isn't as forthcoming with their own apology, you can prompt it by saying something like, "I appreciate you forgiving me. Is there anything you think you could have done better in approaching me in the first place or that you're sorry for?" You should expect some genuine effort from your teen and a sincere apology. If you don't get either from them, tell them that you will be back in a few minutes after they've taken time to really think about their part in the escalation. DO NOT let them out of the break or continue this discussion until you have seen some genuine thoughtfulness and remorse for the behavior that made you insist that they take a break in the first place. Remorse and empathy are two important signs that someone's emotional temperature has dropped and that their thinking brain is back online.

Now that your teen has expressed remorse, discuss how they might have approached you to discuss their concern. Say something like, "I need you to know that I am always willing to hear whatever you have to say to me as long as you can approach me respectfully. Before we address the actual concern that got you so upset in the first place, can you think of how you might have tried to talk to me about this instead of (doing what you did)?"

Don't settle for telling them to avoid being disrespectful. Now is the time to coach your teen on the words they could have used or things they could have done to get your attention in more respectful ways. Be open to the possibility that you have not done a good job of giving them respectful ways to get your attention. Parents often ignore or dismiss their teen's concerns until the teen feels like he or she has no choice but to lash out. Be willing to acknowledge this possibility and work together to develop a way your teen can bring concerns to you and know that he or she will be heard.

Once you've worked out a better way for your teen to express his or her concerns to you, it's finally time to problem-solve the original concern. Do your best not to tell your teen what to do. Use virtue-prompting and other techniques outlined in this book to lead them to the solutions. Your job is to teach your disciple how to think about making good choices. Sometimes your teen will need more direct coaching, but give advice as a last resort. Make them think through their problems using virtues as a guide. Lead them to the best answer. If neither of you know the best answer, acknowledge that and seek appropriate help together.

4. Repeat the Steps as Necessary

The "break" isn't over until you and your teen have walked through all of the above steps. If your teen isn't self-regulated enough to be remorseful/respectful or work with you to find solutions, continue the break and re-engage. Do not let them out of the break until they have successfully worked with you to identify steps for resolving the problem that triggered them in the first place. The goal of this experience is to come out understanding each other better and feeling more confident in your ability to work together. If this process consistently breaks down and/or you consistently come away without good answers for how to move forward, professional counseling help might be indicated. Make the commitment to your family to get the tools you need to help them succeed.

CHAPTER 21

Logical Consequences

L ogical consequences are an important part of effective discipline. A consequence is not a punishment. Punishments simply impose (often random) inconveniences or pain on the child in the belief that, if the child suffers enough for doing "bad" things, they will spontaneously learn to do "good" things.

As opposed to punishments, logical consequences create a system whereby the child must consistently demonstrate good behavior in order to earn — or earn back — a privilege that was abused. Logical consequences are never random, and they're not all that creative. They're tied directly to the offense, and they lead directly to the desired appropriate response. Here are some examples of logical consequences at work:

> Eric is fifteen, and his parents had a rule: no phones at dinner or at family times. Even so, Eric was consistently sneak-texting his friends at dinner or getting distracted by social media notifications when the family was trying to play games or engage in other family time.

> His parents preferred not to be heavy-handed about his phone use. They tried to make sure that there wasn't something serious going on before asking Eric to put his phone away, and each time they reminded him of the rule. Unfortunately, as time went on, Eric was flouting the rule more and more frequently.

His parents decided it was time to take the phone away for at least a week, to give Eric an opportunity to learn to stop taking the family for granted.

They explained the rule: "In this house, we always work hard to love people more than things. But by acting the way you do, you are loving your phone more than you love your family, and that's not okay. We want you to be able to have your phone and use social media, but only if you are mature enough to show us that you can love the people around you more."

Eric's parents explained that he was not going to be allowed to use his phone for a week. During that week, they were going to use virtue-prompting and team-building strategies to help him think of ways he could show his family that he loved them more than he loved his phone or social media. That included behaviors like actively participating in family activities and conversations, and doing his chores and schoolwork to the best of his ability and without being reminded.

Eric's parents explained that they would have a meeting with him at the end of the week. At that time, they would decide whether he had done his best over the last week to show that he loved people more than his things. If he made a genuinely sincere effort, he would be allowed to have the phone back with the understanding that he would need to continue to show that he loved his family more than his phone. On the other hand, if he did not follow through, or did the bare minimum with a bad attitude in the hopes of wearing them down or waiting them out, when they met at the end of the week, Eric would lose the phone for another week to give him a chance to practice loving people more than things.

This consequence was logical for two reasons. First, the punishment (losing the phone) was directly tied to the inappropriate behavior (abusing phone privileges). Second, his parents didn't just take away the phone and expect to have a better kid in seven days. They required him to show that he was mature enough to have the phone by demonstrating the virtues that were missing. Only when he showed his parents that he was able to love the people around him more than he loved the phone that his parents gave him were his parents able to return the phone, with the caveat that Eric keep his priorities straight. This approach eventually helped Eric learn to enjoy technology in a responsible, family-centered way.

Here is another example:

Jen (age sixteen) was being consistently disrespectful to her mother. Most of their arguments happened when Jen's mom attempted to set limits on the amount of time Jen wanted to spend with her friends. Jen's parents were quite generous about this, but they insisted that there were certain family activities — like some family meals, nightly family prayer, and family game night — that Jen needed to be at unless it was a particularly special event (such as homecoming or an activity that she was obliged to participate in). Jen was unwilling to see the difference between these exceptions and any time with her friends, since it was all "important to her." It got to the point that any attempt to set limits on the time Jen spent with her friends resulted in an almost immediate escalation.

After several attempts to address her disrespect gently, including taking a break, Jen's parents decided that they needed to ground her. The point of the grounding was not to punish her for wanting to spend time with her friends. Rather, Jen's parents needed to see that Jen was mature enough to have good balance in her life between her friends and family.

They explained to Jen that she would not be able to go out for at least a week. During that time, she would be expected to be a positive, contributing member of the household. She would be expected to help her parents make dinner and set the table. She would need to be an active and cheerful participant in all family activities. She would need to think of things she could do — on her own — to show the family that she actually cared about them, instead of just treating them as the nuisances she had to put up with when she couldn't be with her friends.

Jen's parents explained that they would not correct her from day to day. If she struggled, they would gently remind her of their deal, but they would not add any additional consequences for the time being. At the end of the week, they would review her effort. If she was truly successful at showing her family that she loved them and wanted to be part of the family, they would trust that she was mature enough to balance her family with her social life. If not, she would be given another week to practice being mature enough to put first things first. It was up to Jen whether this went on for a week or indefinitely. She was in control, and her behavior would be the determining factor.

The first week was horrible. Jen pouted most of the time. She hid in her room. She did what her parents asked her to do, but only if they reminded her, and then with a poor attitude. They did remind her, gently, of what was required to get her social privileges back, but they did not fight with her or add to her punishment when she all but ignored them.

At the end of the week, Jen and her parents met. Jen's parents asked her how she thought the week went. She said, "Fine."

Jen's parents explained that they were disappointed that she showed so little maturity and displayed so little insight now. They asked her again if she truly believed that she did her best to live up to the terms of their agreement. Jen said, "I never agreed. I don't think any of this is fair! You just want to trap me here forever and never let me grow up!"

Jen's dad said, "I'm sorry you feel that way. Obviously that isn't true, but I'm not going to waste time arguing with you. Having a happy life means knowing how to have good balance between your family and your social life. Your response to this whole week says to me that, sadly, you don't have the maturity to balance your friends and family, and I can't let you get away without learning how to do that. You'll be a miserable adult if you don't. I'm giving you another week to practice. We'll review your progress again next week and decide whether you've made enough progress to be allowed to see your friends. I really hope you do well because — regardless of what you think of us — we want you to be able to be with your friends, but we're not going to let you be a monster to the people who love you most. I hope you'll try harder this week."

Of course Jen was furious. She pouted the rest of the day. Her parents were afraid they would have to keep her grounded until she was thirty. Fortunately, the week got better. The next day, Jen started coming around and helping out. By the middle of the week, she was even leading family prayer and suggesting games they could play. They saw her really working to change her attitude, and they complimented her on her efforts throughout the week.

At the end of the second week, Jen sat down with her parents again. They told her that they were proud of the efforts she'd made and that they were going to let her see her friends as long as she continued to show that she could maintain a good balance and a good attitude about family time. Jen agreed. She apologized for her behavior. Her parents went the extra mile and promised that they would always be open to discussing any important conflicts between her social life and her family life. They said they would do their best to be generous, but that they needed to see Jen working with them, not against them. She agreed, and her parents made a point to thank her for working so hard on her attitude and to tell her how proud they were of the maturity she was showing.

Logical consequences — in order to be truly logical — must be tied to the offense and give the teen the guidance/structure necessary to change their behavior. Logical consequences are not meant to be a punishment (even when your child reacts as if it's a punishment). Rather, logical consequences create a structure that enables success.

• • •

Conclusion to Part Three: Closing the Toolbox

Discipleship Parents don't waste their time coming up with ever more creative ways to force their teens to submit to their authority. Instead, they look for ways to create peaceful, orderly interactions within the household that help facilitate the brain-based regulation that's necessary for children to learn and grow in virtue. Discipleship Parents follow Saint John Bosco's example of training their young disciples through the use of "reason, religion, and loving-kindness." They aren't interested in being enforcers or police officers. Rather, Discipleship Parents see themselves as loving shepherds and mentors to their teens, committed to using every encounter to create more loving, joyful households, and more generous, loving, virtuous young adults.

Prayer

Jesus, you are my Good Shepherd. Help me lead my sheep to you with the same gentleness, mercy, kindness, and love with which you shepherd me. Let me be like you, "slow to anger, abounding in mercy." Help me to love and guide my teens down the right paths in a manner that shows them how to be good out of love, not fear. And help me to always remember that discipline is not something I do to my children, but a relationship I have with my children that fills their hearts with your love and makes them want to share that same love with others.

Holy Family, pray for us! Amen.

Discussion Questions

How did the techniques in part 3 challenge your ideas about what effective discipline entails?

How does the approach to discipline outlined in these chapters differ from the way your parents raised you — especially during your teen years?

How could this approach to discipline improve your relationship with your teens?

Which of the techniques described here do you already use? Which would you like to become more effective with?

What behaviors would you most be interested in helping your teens overcome? Which of the techniques do you think would be most helpful and why?

PART FOUR
Discipleship Parenting for the Ages (and Stages)

In this final section, we'll look at what it takes to disciple your children from the preteen years through adolescence.

You'll discover how to parent gracefully through the challenges of each stage, apply the ideas we've discussed to specific discipline challenges, and help your teens meet their needs in godly ways so that they can experience their Catholic faith as the path to a healthy, fulfilling, joyful life.

While you may prefer to zero in on the chapters that focus on the ages of your own children, we encourage you to also look at the chapters that discuss the stages immediately before and after. Developmental stages are somewhat fluid. Some of the information discussed in an earlier stage will most likely apply to your child, while the information discussed in the subsequent chapter will give you a better sense of the goals you are parenting toward.

We hope the following chapters will be a blueprint for building your House of Discipleship with grace and confidence.

CHAPTER 22

Discipling Your Preteen with Grace (Approximately Ages Eleven to Twelve)

*Do not conform yourselves to this age but be transformed
by the renewal of your mind, that you may discern what is
the will of God, what is good and pleasing and perfect.*

Romans 12:2

The preteen years are a period of critical formation. What we do in these few short years lays the groundwork for our child's healthy psycho-sexual and spiritual identity. As the verse that begins this chapter suggests, the primary task of Discipleship Parents during this time is to help their children not to be conformed to the ideas of the world, but formed as authentic Christian persons capable of consistently discerning — with your assistance — God's will for their lives and relationships.

Recall the House of Discipleship, which we first introduced in chapter 8. As you can see in the graphic, ideally, each stage builds on the strengths, virtues, and lessons learned in the one before it.

House of Discipleship

Stage Four: Relational Discipleship (Adolescence)

Teen turns toward parent to develop skills for having godly relationships and finding place in world.

Stage Three: Vocational Discipleship (Middle Childhood)

Child turns toward parent to discover and develop gifts in a way that helps him glorify God and make meaningful contributions to family and others.

Stage Two: Foundational Discipleship (Early Childhood)

Child turns toward parent to learn the stories, rules, and structures that lead to a love-filled, well-ordered life.

Stage One: Embodied Discipleship (Infancy and Toddlerhood)

Child turns toward parent to learn self-regulation and empathy through body-to-body communication.

The preteen years are a time for children to master the skills of middle childhood and begin practicing some of the skills that will need to be cultivated in adolescence. Some preteens need more time to cultivate the skills of middle childhood, while others will begin taking on the early challenges of adolescence. Either way, it is good for parents to make sure their preteens have developed the personal and social skills necessary to enter adolescence confidently, without allowing them to rush ahead. A twelve-year-old can seem especially mature — especially if they are the oldest — but there are still significant differences in mental ability between a twelve-year-old and a fourteen- or sixteen-year-old. In the preteen years, outward signs of psychological maturity may not be as deeply rooted as appearances might suggest. Parents need to be sensitive to this fact.

Discipleship Parents will need to spend this relatively brief period of time (ages eleven through twelve) laying down a foundation for their children to understand how to start using their gifts and talents to benefit others. They will also make sure to strengthen the preteen's healthy connections to the family while simultaneously making room for more meaningful social connections outside the home.

As preteens move into adolescence, Discipleship Parents need to focus on showing them how their faith and moral vision can help them develop healthy, meaningful, godly relationships and discover God's plan for their place in the world.

All this said, you aren't too late if you just start Discipleship Parenting with your preteen. Kids of every age respond well to Discipleship Parenting approaches. The hardest part of making a shift from more conventional parenting approaches to Discipleship Parenting is the change in mindset required by you.

Although we don't recommend it for any stage, for children younger than ten, parents can get away with a "do what I say because I said so" approach to parenting. By the time children hit eleven, though, many kids will start to push back against this approach. This isn't defiance or disrespect, and if you respond to it as if it is, the years ahead will result in an escalating battle of wills. The resistance preteens and teens have to just being told what to do accompanies their ability to think and reason at a deeper level. With preteens and teens, resistance usually means, "I don't understand how to do what you're asking me to do and still meet my needs. I need you to help me connect the dots." In this case, connecting the dots means more than telling them what to do. It means asking leading questions that help them identify their needs, discover possible obstacles, talk through their concerns, and brainstorm ways to address those needs while still being compliant and respectful to your wishes and needs.

Discipline should be a collaborative dialogue between the mentor (parent) and disciple (child) at every age and stage, but as we move closer to adolescence, this dialogue becomes critical. The more your teens see you as an obstacle to meeting their needs, the more pushback and resistance you are going to get. Fortunately, this is an entirely avoidable dynamic. You don't have to say yes to every request in order to maintain rapport. You just have to convey — in both your words and your attitude — that "I am on your side. I am committed to helping you fulfill your obligations AND meet your needs. Let's figure it out together." The more you can effectively maintain this balance between insisting that your needs are important and validating your children's needs, the less resistance you will get and the quicker you'll be able to overcome whatever resistance does arise.

Maintaining Attachment with Your Preteen
There are three important practices Discipleship Parents need to maintain in order to keep secure attachment with their preteens: strong family rituals, attentive listening, and the qualified yes technique.

Strong Family Rituals
In the preteen (and teen) years, it becomes more tempting than ever to abandon family rituals and routines in favor of a hundred different extracurricular activities and social obligations. In truth, while some flexibility can be necessary, strong family routines and rituals are critical for the well-being of every preteen, and maintaining strong family rituals for working, playing, talking, and praying together (including regular one-on-one time) is key to maintaining attachment with your preteen. Family rituals are not just a way of keeping your family together. They model how Christians relate to work, leisure, relationships, and faith.

When families make *daily* time to work, play, talk, and pray together (even briefly), their values toward these categories of activity become communicated implicitly and are translated into a preteen's muscle memory. Like the current in a river, strong rituals and routines (bedtimes, mealtimes, regular days for chores, etc.) establish the flow in your household that carries everyone along. If you have established this flow, conversations about faith, values, and responsibilities simply confirm what your preteen is already experiencing in his daily life. When you talk about why working together and being a team is important, you're simply filling in the cognitive blanks for something he or she has already experienced as true because of the fruit borne of your daily household working-together rituals. When you discuss why some ways to have fun are healthier and more fulfilling than others, you're simply helping your child intellectually appreciate what he or she has already experienced in all the daily play rituals your family has established. When you have conversations about why you need to take better care of one another and be more sensitive to each other's feelings, you are simply putting flesh on the bones of what your child has already encountered in all the conversations you've had in your family talk rituals. When you share about all the ways God and faith touch on every aspect of life, you are simply helping your preteen wrap their head around concepts they have already experienced time and again in your daily family prayer rituals.

Conversations about faith, values, and proper behavior held in the context of strong family rituals and routines provide confirmation of everything your preteen is already experiencing in the actual life of your family. Conversations only become tension-filled lectures when your preteen has not seen the concepts you are espousing at work in your household.

Attentive Listening

Just as plants thrive when they are given sun, water, and fertilizer, preteens and teens thrive when they feel truly listened to. Some kids open up more readily than others. Some kids need more encouragement and coaching than others. But you should never make the mistake of thinking that your preteen's struggle to open up means they do not want to talk with you or are not dying to be heard by you.

Don't save conversation time with your preteens and teens until *you* need to say something to them. A good rule of thumb is that you should spend 80 to 90 percent more time listening to your kids talking to you than you spend talking to them. That's going to require three things:

- Establishing regular one-on-one time
- Asking good questions
- Letting them lead/teach

Preteens and teens need time to figure out what they want to say and how to say it. They need time to focus on you, their feelings, and the words they need to use to get things out the right way. They cannot do this in fifteen minutes in your car on the way to practice when they are worried about how they're going to perform and you're already thinking about what you need to get done after you drop them off. You need to have at least an hour, preferably several times a week, where you and your child can be in the same space.

Pope Francis encouraged parents to "waste time" with their kids. Similarly, in his book *The Seven Levels of Intimacy*, Catholic author Matthew Kelly speaks of "carefree timelessness." Whatever the language you use, the concept is the same. Relationships require a regular investment of time. The reality is, what/who you treasure is represented by what/who you invest your time in. Implicitly, your kids know whether you really treasure them or not. The more they know you treasure them — because you're willing to put the time into a relationship with them — the more they will open up to you and be open to your influence when the time comes to share it.

The previous points about family rituals come into play here as well. Without an established date-time ritual with your kids, it is hard to maintain the level of connection you need to capture their hearts and disciple them. Create regularly scheduled times when you connect one-on-one over breakfast or a shared activity (like a walk or project) and use the time to listen to whatever they want to discuss.

Second, ask good questions. Don't just say, "How was your day?" Say, "What's going on in that situation with so-and-so?" or "How are things working out with this-and-that?" or even, "What do you think about thus-and-such?" It's okay to ask leading questions like we discussed in the discipleship discipline section on virtue-prompting, but it's even better just to ask gentle, open-ended questions that help you get to know your kids' minds. A great resource for this is the classic book, *How To Talk So Teens Will Listen and Listen So Teens Will Talk* (Faber and Mazlish).

Third, look for opportunities to let them teach you. Find things they know more about than you or are better at than you and ask them to tell you about it — or better still, teach you what they know. Your ability to model humility and a willingness to learn goes a long way toward helping your kids be willing to listen to and learn from you.

The Qualified Yes Technique

Sometimes we need to say no to our kids. Whenever they are asking for permission to do something where there is a clear and present danger (as opposed to a vaguely possible concern rooted more in our anxiety than reality), it is important that we be willing to set firm limits. For everything else, the qualified yes technique is a useful tool.

When our kids ask for something that we are not able to give, or that we would be willing to give but are concerned that they aren't mature enough to handle, the qualified yes technique allows us to set reasonable parameters around our kids' actions without shutting them down.

For instance, if your kid asks for something you simply can't afford, you might say, "Well, I might be able to give you X toward that, but if it's really important to you, you would have to find a way to make up the difference. I would be willing to help you make a plan, but it would be up to you to do it. What do you think?"

In this example, the parent isn't shutting their preteen/teen down. They aren't even questioning their kid's judgment. Instead, they are showing that they are willing to help their kid meet their goals. It's now up to the child to determine whether the thing they wanted is really worth working toward or not. This is actually a terrific exercise because it helps kids learn to identify what is worth working for and what isn't. Setting and meeting goals is an important part of self-esteem. Your willingness to help them with this process is a tremendous way to build rapport.

You can also use the qualified yes technique when your preteen asks for a privilege that you aren't sure he is ready for. Instead of saying, "You can't do that until you're sixteen," and then living to regret it when your sixteen-year-old is no more mature than he was at twelve, you might say, "I would like you to be able to do that because it would mean that you were (insert qualities/virtues). I think you're getting there, but I'm not sure you're there yet. Let's come up with a plan to help you develop those (qualities/virtues) so that you can be confident that you could really handle yourself in that situation."

The perfectly legitimate reason we often say no to our kids' request for privileges is that we are concerned that they would not be able to handle the responsibility well. Rather than just saying no or taking an unfounded risk, the qualified yes technique allows us to voice our concern and enlist our kids' support in addressing it. What would they need to do to be able to handle that responsibility well? Would they need to display more self-control, attentiveness, responsibility, faithfulness, etc.? What clear, concrete behaviors would your preteen need to display before you could be confident that they could handle the privileges/responsibilities/ opportunities they are requesting — *in a healthy and godly way*? Make a plan with your preteen to develop those qualities around the house or in their relationship with you or their siblings and let them know that you can revisit their request when they have shown progress in this area.

The genius of this technique is that it changes the conversation from "When are my parents finally going to cave and how can I wear them down?" to "What do I have to do to show them that I've developed the virtues they need to see in me to know that I could handle myself well?" The former question leads to a battle of wills; the latter question leads to an ongoing discussion about maturity and character development.

The qualified yes technique helps you avoid unnecessary fights with your kids while still enabling you to set appropriate parameters on their behavior and demonstrate that you are on their side. Remember, attachment is the gut-level sense your kids have that you are the person to whom your kids can confidently turn to get what they need to lead an abundant life. This technique enhances attachment by demonstrating to your kids that you want to play a part in getting everything they need to have a fulfilling life and being able to handle it well once they get it.

Taken together, strong family rituals, attentive listening strategies, and the qualified yes technique help you maintain attachment with your child through the preteen and adolescent years. Each, in its own way, allows you to communicate to your child that you are the person to whom they can turn to get the answers, resources, and support they need to lead a fulfilling life.

Developmental Challenges for Preteens

The preteen years bridge the gap between middle childhood and adolescence. In the House of Discipleship Model (see below) the preteen years are primarily concerned with putting the finishing touches on the tasks associated with vocational discipleship, with an eye toward setting the stage for the process of relational discipleship characterized by the teen years. In light of this, many preteens may be dealing with the middle childhood issues we discussed in *Parenting Your Kids with Grace (Birth to age 10)*. If your preteens tend to be somewhat less mature members of their peer group in terms of their communication skills, ability to appropriately express emotions, handle responsibilities at school or home, or demonstrate good initiative and leadership skills, you might find it helpful to review the chapter on middle childhood in that book.

Of course, pre-adolescence is its own developmental stage and brings with it some unique discipleship opportunities for you and your child. They include:

- Continuing to foster emotional maturity
- Encouraging mastery of "industry"
- Fostering transition from story and structure stage of spiritual life
- Fostering healthy sexual and social identity

Fostering Emotional Maturity

Emotional maturity comes from the ability to maintain our emotional temperature especially when we aren't feeling well or when we are dealing with stressful situations. We cannot control emotions directly. We can't just "calm down" or "be happy." But we can intentionally slow down our thoughts, speech, and actions. We can take a deep breath

House of Discipleship

Stage Four: Relational Discipleship (Adolescence)

Teen turns toward parent to develop skills for having godly relationships and finding place in world.

Stage Three: Vocational Discipleship (Middle Childhood)

Child turns toward parent to discover and develop gifts in a way that helps him glorify God and make meaningful contributions to family and others.

Stage Two: Foundational Discipleship (Early Childhood)

Child turns toward parent to learn the stories, rules, and structures that lead to a love-filled, well-ordered life.

Stage One: Embodied Discipleship (Infancy and Toddlerhood)

Child turns toward parent to learn self-regulation and empathy through body-to-body communication.

when we feel stressed. We can take a pause before responding. We can pray or reflect before acting. All of these intentional actions — and others like them — help us learn to consciously manage our emotional temperatures and feel our feelings without being ruled by them.

Even so, the preteen years present real challenges to a child's ability to learn healthy emotional management habits such as these. Discipleship Parents need to be particularly sensitive to the increased presence of hormones and the more socially complex environment that preteens are forced to contend with, all of which make learning to manage one's emotional temperature not impossible, but certainly more difficult.

We don't have space in this book to deal with all the varieties of challenges preteens face. Fortunately, we don't have to. The more *both* parents and preteens are able to practice keeping their emotional temperatures at a 6 or lower, the more capable they will be of responding well to almost any situation.

Keeping one's emotional temperature at a 6 or lower does not mean that you or your child never get upset, or that you are always perfectly calm and polite with each other. What it does mean is that you and your child are actively working to recognize that, in healthy people, emotions are not a call to action. Rather, they are a call to prayer and planning.

Many people have the wrong idea about emotions. Some have been led to believe that every emotion must be acted upon immediately; on the other hand, others believe that emotions must be repressed because of their destructive potential. Both approaches are unhealthy and tend to lead to anxiety and depressive disorders as well as a host of relationship and social problems.

There is an alternative to these unhealthy approaches to managing our emotions, and while emotional maturity is a lifelong project, the ideal time for laying the foundation for this skill is pre-adolescence, when feelings are right on the surface and there are plenty of opportunities to practice.

Saint Paul writes, "We destroy arguments and every pretension raising itself against the knowledge of God, and take every thought captive in obedience to Christ" (2 Cor 10:4–5). Our emotions are a gift from God. We don't need to fear them, and we need not be slaves to them. Because original sin disrupted the order God created in the world, our emotions — like everything else in the world — don't work the way God created them to. They are often "out of order," so to speak. As Saint Paul suggests, our job as Christians is to bring our feelings to God so that he can teach us how to respond to them.

Pre-adolescence is a good time to begin teaching this skill, although you should be patient and take the long view on this process. Let your child mature into this with your gentle guidance and support. The following steps will help foster emotional mastery.

1. Take Your Own and Your Child's Emotional Temperature Throughout the Day

Model good emotional management by using the chapter on the emotional temperature scale to talk about the emotional temperatures in your household. Based solely on the behavioral markers (instead of just going by how you think you feel), share your emotional temperature throughout the day in a casual, conversational manner. "I think I'm at a 4 this morning. How about you?" Or, "That was really stressful. I think I almost got up to an 8. I had to do X to try to keep my cool. What did your emotional temperature get to?" Or, "I'm in an okay mood, but this headache/cold/upset stomach is really pushing me up to a 7. I appreciate you guys being a little quieter and kinder to each other today, even more than usual."

You can't master what you aren't paying attention to. Most people just ignore their feelings until they can't ignore them anymore. Talking about your emotional temperature and encouraging your kids to do the same helps them become consciously aware of their stress level and what they need to do to manage it.

2. Empathize and Pray

When our kids are upset, we tend to try one of two things. Either we try to talk them out of their feelings ("You shouldn't feel that way! There are lots of good things about you! You have lots of friends!"); or we get angry with them for feeling less than happy ("What do *you* have to be upset about?" "You better watch your attitude!" "I'm so sick of you moping around all the time!")

The best way to help your kids learn to manage their strong feelings

— especially their strong negative feelings — is to empathize and then help your child bring their feelings to God. For example, if your child is struggling with a situation at school, instead of trying to talk them out of it, you might say, "I'm really sorry you're going through that. It really hurts when friends don't include us." Or, "I know how disappointed you are. It's frustrating to get a lower grade than you were hoping for."

Be careful not to come off as patronizing or placating, which is what happens when we are not as interested in really understanding our child's emotions as we are in wanting them to "get over it." Instead, work to sincerely and attentively make your teen feel understood by actually trying to understand and appreciate their experience through their eyes.

You can continue the conversation in this vein for a bit. When your child gives you some indication (verbally or nonverbally) that they feel like you understand their feelings (i.e., you have collected them), lead them in bringing the situation to God in prayer. Specifically, ask God to help you and your child discern how he wants you to respond to this feeling and the situation that provoked it. For instance, "Lord, James is really having a hard time not beating up on himself for failing the quiz today. Help him to know how much you love him and how much I love him. And help us to work together to make a plan to help him do better next time."

3. Reduce the Temperature
When we are upset about something, we immediately want to rush ahead to the part where we solve the problem. Unfortunately, this often results in us doing impulsive things that make our situations worse.

Once you have collected your child by empathizing and praying with them, reflect together on some simple things he or she could do (alone or with you) that would help reduce their emotional temperature by at least one or two points. Do they need another hug? Would they like to take some time to read, take a walk, or pray on their own? It's okay to share what you do to take your emotional temperature down in situations like this, as long you don't turn it into a lecture.

The goal is to help your child get their emotional temperature down to a 5 or lower so that their thinking brain can come back online and they can figure out the healthiest way to respond to the emotionally charged situation moving forward.

4. Plan

Having connected with your child, helped them bring the situation to God, and coached them through calming down enough to bring their thinking brain back online, it's time to make a plan. Help your child understand that we are not meant to merely suffer our emotions. Feelings are meant to alert us to a need to do something different. Lead your child through the process of coming up with a plan for handling a similar situation better next time. You can use the virtue-prompting technique to help guide the conversation. For instance, "If you had to handle that situation with your friends again, what virtues or strengths do you think you'd need to handle it well? What would you do differently if you could show those virtues or strengths next time?"

Not only does this process model a healthier way to manage emotions, but it also teaches your child to see the opportunity for spiritual and personal growth that is contained within every setback.

Many adults struggle to use this process for managing their own emotional reactions, much less their kids'. It's okay if you are one of them. This is just one more example of how Discipleship Parenting can be healing for us too. If you struggle with anxiety, anger, sadness, or any other feeling-problem, and you see your child having similar struggles, one powerful technique is to ask your child to work with you to help each other manage that feeling better. You don't want to make your child responsible for being your therapist, but it's more than okay to say to your child, "Sometimes I have a hard time handling my anger/sadness/fear/etc. appropriately. It looks like you struggle with that sometimes too. Why don't we help each other out?" Propose a way for you and your child to empathize, pray, reduce, and plan together when one of you sees the other falling into that particular emotional trap. This is a much healthier approach than allowing your emotional reactions to feed off of each other and create tension and alienation in the household. Kids at this age tend to flourish when they are given age-appropriate responsibility for doing their part to help maintain good relations in the household.

Encourage Mastery of "Industry"

Middle school children are focused on learning "industry" (the ability to set and meet goals), which is a key ingredient of healthy self-esteem.

If your child hasn't been involved in some kind of activity that challenges him or her to grow and interact with peers who have similar interests — music lessons, sports, dance, etc. — pre-adolescence is really a critical period for this. Beyond this point, you will have to drag your child to do any meaningful activity. Once the window closes on the time frame to learn industry, it can be very difficult to motivate your child to become involved in any activity that remotely challenges them to develop their gifts, especially around their peers.

Your child doesn't have to be a master of a particular skill or have a passion for something before you enroll them in an activity or lessons of some kind. This is the time in life when kids should be given a chance to try different things. It matters less what they do than that they are given the chance to stick with something until they develop some basic skills. If a child doesn't enjoy a particular activity, set a goal with them and let them withdraw after that goal is met (for instance, attaining their next belt, or after the recital, or at the end of the season). That said, don't let your child quit something without choosing another activity to take its place. Sitting at home staring at screens of one sort or another is not an acceptable option. Your preteen needs opportunities to challenge him- or herself and interact with other peers who have interests and passions. If this isn't happening by now, you will need to make it a priority.

Some parents are rightly concerned with overscheduling their kids. This is where strong family rituals come in. If you choose activities that don't compete (too much) with strong family rituals for working, playing, talking, and praying together, you will be able to strike that balance between getting your child involved in meaningful activities without losing your child to those activities. There will always be some tension here, but the tension is good. The real problems come when kids land too far on one side or the other — either being too involved in activities or not being involved in anything.

Fostering Transition from Story and Structure Stage of Spiritual Life

Spiritually speaking, the middle school years are characterized by the stories and structures stage of faith development. In the years from ages six to ten, children's spiritual lives revolve around learning stories that help them understand good versus evil, heroism versus cowardice, virtues versus vices, etc. Having a regular reading time ritual during which you share and discuss not only Bible and saint stories, but also good children's literature that helps kids learn to think critically, is tremendously important. If Mom and Dad aren't regularly sharing stories with their children, they are ceding their authority as meaning-makers and worldview-shapers to TV, the internet, and secular culture.

Developmentally speaking, kids in both middle childhood (ages six to ten) and the preteen years (ages eleven to twelve) are also concerned with learning the rules, structures, and habits that will help them be good people and contribute in a positive way to their family, their church, and their school. We discuss this stage in greater detail in both *Parenting Your Kids with Grace (Birth to age 10)* and *Discovering God Together: The Catholic Guide to Raising Faithful Kids*. Because preteens still have a foot in the middle childhood years, it would be useful to review these resources for additional information.

Beyond this, preteens are ready to start understanding the gray that often exists between black and white, legitimate versus illegitimate exceptions to rules, and how two competing or contrasting ideas can be true at the same time. For instance, in your nightly reading time ritual or family prayer time ritual, you might read the Parable of the Prodigal Son. In this parable, the father runs to forgive his wayward son. Contrast this with the Parable of the Unmerciful Servant, in which the king throws his wayward servant in prison. After you read these superficially contradictory stories, you might discuss how, if both are true, what is each saying about mercy? How does each story inform or shape our understanding of the other?

These kinds of conversations about the stories, structures, and rules that make up the Christian worldview help kids apply these insights to the real world. Discipleship Parents understand that making time for these kinds of conversations helps kids connect the dots between the way things should be and the way things are. Unfortunately, research by the Center for Applied Research in the Apostolate (CARA) at Georgetown University and Holy Cross Family Ministries found that more than 70 percent of Catholic parents have not had a conversation about faith or values with their children in the last month. When parents do not have these conversations, kids often experience faith crises and even loss of faith. They confront situations in their relationships with family, friends, and even themselves that don't fit neatly into the little boxes they were given in childhood, so they decide that their faith has nothing relevant to say about the complexities of real life. There is a reason another study by CARA found that most children lose their faith between the ages of eleven and thirteen. Unless Catholic parents take their role as meaning-makers and worldview-shapers seriously, their children's faith will most likely go dormant. Worse, most parents don't even notice their kid's faith has been on life support for most of their adolescence. They miss every clue until their children stop going to church in college. Don't let this happen to your kids. Share and discuss biblical stories, the lives of the saints, and even contemporary fiction and movies. Use media to explore with your child (as opposed to lecturing at your child) why some worldviews are healthier and godlier than others.

Of course, as important as regular faith conversations are, religion isn't an academic subject. It is a relationship. We meet Christ in prayer. Many Catholic teens lose their faith in Christ because they have never actually met him. Again, the study on family spirituality by CARA/HCFM found that only 17 percent of Catholic families regularly pray together. It is not enough to simply drag our preteens to church, religious ed, or youth groups. These things exist to foster an already existing relationship with Christ that families have developed in their homes through meaningful family prayer. Taking our kids to these very important activities without first having introduced them to Christ in our homes is a bit like trying to start a fire by piling up kindling without ever lighting a match. In *Parenting Your Kids with Grace* and *Discovering God Together*, we offer many tips for creating a meaningful prayer time where families can encounter Christ at home.

Hopefully your family has been praying together since your children were babies. If so, your preteens will be more than ready to take turns leading prayer, giving blessings to you and their siblings (as well as receiving blessings), and making important contributions to faith conversations. It's important to encourage their spiritual leadership. Having seen Mom and Dad model different ways to pray meaningfully — i.e., not just saying words at God, but actively inviting God into our lives through whatever prayer forms we might prefer to use — gently encourage your preteens to take spiritual initiative. Ask them to pray for you (and with you, and over you) when you are having a challenging day. When they have something to celebrate, remind them to thank God and join them in prayer in the moment, but ask them to lead. When they are going through a frustrating time, remind them to ask for God's help and guidance and join them in prayer in the moment, but ask them to lead.

If you haven't been praying regularly as a family, it isn't too late to start, but it is imperative that you start now. The longer you wait to start praying as a family — especially past ten years old — the more resistance and pushback you can expect. That isn't a reason not to persist in making family prayer a habit, but if you have the opportunity to start sooner rather than later, you will make your life that much easier. A simple way to get started is to use the PRAISE format for family prayer that we outlined in chapter 1. We also offer additional tips for making family prayer meaningful in *Discovering God Together*.

Fostering Healthy Sexual/Social Identity

In addition to the preteen years being a critical period for fostering a more mature spiritual life, pre-adolescence is an important time for helping your kids develop a healthy sexual/social identity. There are three primary lessons Discipleship Parents must teach to foster healthy sexual and social identity in the preteen years and beyond.

1. Foster an authentic understanding of masculinity/femininity.
2. Foster an understanding of the different types of love AND the passions that are rightly associated with each type of love.
3. Foster a healthy sense of friendship between boys and girls.

Our book *Beyond the Birds and the Bees* offers a comprehensive look at what Discipleship Parents can do to pass on the Catholic vision of love and foster healthy sexual development from birth through adolescence. Because this process actually begins long before your children reach the preteen years, we strongly encourage readers with children of every age to take advantage of the insights *Beyond the Birds and the Bees* can offer. That said, the following points are some of the more important tasks parents of preteens and teens must keep in mind.

1. Foster an authentic understanding of masculinity/femininity.
All the lessons about sexual and social identity we discussed in the middle childhood chapters of *Parenting Your Kids with Grace* apply here as well. To recap, many parents create serious problems for themselves and their children by adopting worldly attitudes about what it means to be a man or a woman. It is a mistake to treat masculinity or femininity as something that has to be earned or proven. You aren't a boy because you like certain things, prefer doing certain things, and have certain interests. You aren't a girl because you like other things, prefer doing different things, and have certain other interests. These superficial attitudes toward sexual identity make many boys and girls feel tremendously insecure if they don't fit into the categories their parents or society in general tries to stuff them into.

Saint John Paul's Theology of the Body asserts that masculinity or femininity is a God-given gift. Our masculine or feminine identity isn't earned or achieved. It is a fact. It is given. We do our children a grave disservice when we implicitly or explicitly tell them that they must act a certain way, like certain things, or accomplish certain tasks before they can be called a man or woman.

It is good to encourage our children to become more confident in their masculinity or femininity, but that is different than making them prove that they are "man enough" or "woman enough." Our children become more confident in the gifts of their masculinity or femininity when we give them opportunities to use their bodies, minds, gifts, and talents to work for the good of others. As young men use the various gifts God has given them to bless others — whether or not those gifts and talents fit neatly into worldly stereotypes — they become more confident in their masculinity. When young women do the same, they become more confident in their femininity. Boys and girls should never be made to feel that they must prove that they are worthy to be called men or women. Rather, Discipleship Parents should give their kids ample opportunities to exercise their God-given masculinity or femininity by being encouraged to find little ways to serve their family, their Church, their school, and their communities. Masculinity and femininity are the natural fruit that grows on the tree of loving, embodied service of our neighbor.

2. Foster an understanding of the different types of love AND the passions that are rightly associated with each type of love.

In addition to affirming your children's God-given masculinity or femininity, a second important dimension of fostering healthy sexual identity is discussing with your preteens the different types of love that exist and the different passions that are associated with those loves.

For instance:

- *Agape* is both a love of God and a godly love that seeks the ultimate good of others without any interest in getting anything in return.
- *Eros* is the romantic love that, properly expressed, brings forth new life and enables two people to help each other become everything God created them to be over the course of a lifetime together.
- *Filios* is the brotherly and sisterly love that we share with good friends, where we each truly want the best for one another and work hard to help one another be our best selves in every situation.
- *Storge* (STOR-gay) is the love we have for our family members, our team, our school, or our country. It is the pride and warmth we feel toward the groups we belong to and the desire to do our part to help the people in those groups be their best and be well-regarded by others.

While all these different types of love have a different flavor, they all have one thing in common: They are all ordered toward working for the good of someone other than yourself. True love of all the above kinds does feel good and does benefit us, but in each case, the people involved are more concerned about *what they can do for one another* than what they can get out of one another.

Along with an understanding of the different types of love, it's helpful for kids to understand that *there are different passions associated with each of these types of love.* It is a sad fact that the secular world mistakenly and erroneously sexualizes all forms of passion. If you ache to be near someone (or something), miss them when they are gone, feel excited when you think of them, can't wait to share something with them, or experience a strong bond, or even find someone attractive on some level, the world says that this passion must always represent some kind of sexual connection. This is a tremendously narrow and impoverished view of passion. In fact, this view was largely unheard of before the last fifty years of human history. Historically, it was understood that each type of love we described above has a particular passion associated with it, and of the many types of passions that exist, only one is sexual.

The passion associated with agape love is *ecstasy.* Many saints have described the all-consuming fire of love that burns within them and makes them ache to be in God's presence or do heroically virtuous acts — even giving their life — to work for the good of others.

The passion associated with filial love is *friendship.* That might seem like a cheap word in today's usage, but Jesus himself said, "Greater love has no man than to lay down his life for a friend." It is not only possible, but healthy, to find a friend you feel so close to that you miss them when they're gone, ache to see them again, can't wait to share things with them, and feel a connection that goes beyond the connection you feel with most others. Intense experiences of filial love are deeply passionate and completely platonic. The love between Jesus and John, David and Jonathan, or Ruth and Naomi in the Bible is an excellent example. In each of these relationships, the filial love that was shared inspired the friends to build and serve a mission together and sacrifice for each other's greater good. In popular literature, the love between Anne Shirley and her "kindred spirit" Diana Barry in *Anne of Green Gables,* or the love between Frodo and Samwise in *Lord of the Rings,* are good and relatable examples of this same dynamic of platonic, filial passion. Each of these examples of filial passion represented the connection between two people who really "got" each other. This kind of platonic, passionate connection is a real gift to any two people who experience it and should never be cheapened by ascribing sexual dimensions to it.

The passion associated with erotic love is *romantic/sexual passion.*

This is the passion that makes men and women want to give their whole lives to each other and raise children together. Romantic passion is more than a momentary feeling (the term for momentary romantic/sexual passion is "limerence," which refers to the feeling of being romantically addicted to someone). True romantic/sexual passion involves the deeply felt desire for both *lifelong* and *life-giving* love. It is a passion that longs to create something more (i.e., a child) than the lovers could ever be on their own.

Finally, the passion associated with storge is *devotion.* This is the love, fealty, and pride that a parent has for a child, or that a person has for his country or tribe or team.

The world seeks to sexualize every type of passion, robbing us of the many different aspects of love. But Christians understand that the God who came so that we might have life and live it more abundantly wants his people to experience all the different types of passion fully — appreciating the gifts that each can contribute to a rich and fulfilling life. In a world that communicates so many confusing and conflicting messages about love and passion, it is more important than ever for Discipleship Parents to help their children — and especially our preteens and teens — understand the different types of love and passion they might be feeling. By doing so, we can help our children fully appreciate the bounty of love God lays out before them.

3. Foster a healthy sense of friendship between boys and girls.

The last point we will make in this section on fostering sexual and social identity is the need to give our children opportunities to develop healthy friendship groups that involve both young men and young women.

Up until this point, most younger children will gravitate toward same-sex friendships. As children move into the preteen years, it is a good idea to give our children opportunities to join groups, clubs, and activities that involve both genders so that they can learn to see the opposite sex as people and friends before they begin to view them as potential romantic partners.

Secular society seeks not only to sexualize all forms of love and passion, but to sexualize our children at younger and younger ages. The idea that an eleven-year-old (or younger) should or could have a healthy boyfriend or girlfriend relationship is developmentally absurd. Encouraging this idea in any way is offensive to the degree of maturity preteens are capable of.

Preteens who have not been taught the healthy lessons of masculinity/femininity, love and passion, and other developmental lessons will behave in romantically and even sexually precocious ways — not because they want to but because they think they are expected to. We are not suggesting that Discipleship Parents should fear the idea of their teens dating or treat it as a taboo subject. In fact, Discipleship Parenting is primarily about teaching our children how to have healthy, godly, fulfilling relationships of all kinds. But we are saying that encouraging a child to think of an opposite-sex peer in romantic terms before they have been taught to relate to an opposite-sex peer as a truly good friend is a disaster in the making.

By involving your preteens in appropriately supervised, mixed-gender groups that focus around particular activities and interests, you are giving your children the opportunity to see that opposite-sex peers are people just like them. Boys and girls are not mysterious, alien creatures who exist to hook up with. They are human beings with feelings, hopes, and dreams; good qualities and bad qualities; gifts and talents; and all the rest. A person of any age is simply incapable of having a healthy romantic relationship until they have learned that opposite-sex persons are not beings from another planet, but persons much like themselves. Give your preteens the gift of learning to think of the opposite gender as human beings and friends so that, one day, they can build a truly fulfilling romantic relationship with someone who is capable of being a true partner to them.

Conclusion

The preteen years represent a bridge between childhood and adolescence. These years give Discipleship Parents the opportunity to reflect what qualities each particular child will need to develop in order to handle the psychological, emotional, relational, and spiritual challenges of adolescence well.

By the time their children are ten, Discipleship Parents should start transitioning — as is appropriate to the maturity of their particular child

— from a more active teaching role to a mentoring role, where they focus more on modeling, asking leading questions that help their child learn to think independently, and spending time working, playing, talking, and praying together while encouraging the child to take more of a leadership role in these areas.

Many parents are set up to fear the teen years, but in our experience, these years can be the most rewarding years of your parenting career. Parents cannot control every variable, and they shouldn't even try. But as our kids mature, they are able to be more active participants in the discipleship relationship with us. The more successful we are at making the transition from teacher to mentor, the more dynamic the parent-teen relationship becomes and the more exciting it is to watch the sparks of insight we've been tending catch fire.

Prayer

Lord, help me be a good mentor to my preteen. Help me to see these years as an opportunity to prepare them to face the challenges of adolescence with confidence, faith, and virtue. Help me to accompany my child through these years and let them experience me as a support rather than a hindrance to becoming everything you created them to be. Calm my nerves. Steel my courage. Open my heart to the heart of my child so that I can continue to lead them to your heart.

Discussion Questions

How is God using your relationship with your preteen to help you draw closer to him?

What ideas did you find most useful in this chapter? What ideas challenged you?

How will you use the things you learned in this chapter to strengthen your relationship with your preteen?

CHAPTER 23

Discipling Your Teen with Grace (Approximately Ages Thirteen to Eighteen)

Be not afraid!

Saint John Paul

It's probably safe to say that most parents experience a little fear and trepidation when they think of their kids becoming teens. Even so, we would join Saint John Paul in asking our readers to "Be not afraid!"

Adolescence certainly has its challenges, but as a Discipleship Parent, you don't have to be afraid because — as we pointed out earlier — it isn't all up to you. You don't have to have all the answers. You don't have to try to keep your child under lock and key. And you don't have to worry about all the worldly influences at the door. Instead of trying to control all the variables outside of your control, your primary job will be to focus on doing your best to consciously and intentionally invite Christ into every interaction with your teen so that they can know that God is walking

House of Discipleship

Stage Four: Relational Discipleship (Adolescence)

Teen turns toward parent to develop skills for having godly relationships and finding place in world.

Stage Three: Vocational Discipleship (Middle Childhood)

Child turns toward parent to discover and develop gifts in a way that helps him glorify God and make meaningful contributions to family and others.

Stage Two: Foundational Discipleship (Early Childhood)

Child turns toward parent to learn the stories, rules, and structures that lead to a love-filled, well-ordered life.

Stage One: Embodied Discipleship (Infancy and Toddlerhood)

Child turns toward parent to learn self-regulation and empathy through body-to-body communication.

with you and them every step of the way. That's a big enough job all by itself, and no one expects you to do it perfectly. But if you can make that task your primary focus, God will help you and your teen navigate the challenges of adolescence with grace and goodwill.

Discipling Your Teen

As we discussed, the preteen years are still mainly concerned with the vocational discipleship challenges of the late middle school years, and the relational discipleship of the early teen years. Adolescence, on the other hand, is primarily concerned with what we will call "relational discipleship."

Relational Discipleship

In addition to the obvious need to foster healthy attitudes toward opposite-sex peers, relational discipleship is concerned with fostering your teen's healthy relationship with their body, with their family, with God, and with their place in the world.

As we mentioned in the last chapter, while we do not recommend it at any stage, parents can more or less get away with "because I said so" approaches to parenting children who are younger than ten. Over that age, such approaches tend to lead down one of two unhealthy paths. Either the teen will act like a "good boy/girl" because they are afraid of offending the parent but, because they haven't really been taught to think for themselves, will be poorly equipped to make healthy personal, relational, or moral choices once they leave the house; or the parent and teen will become caught up in a vortex of tension and conflict that escalates throughout the teen years and can lead to a host of unpredictable and undesirable consequences in the child's life and the parent-child relationship.

If a parent has not overcome their tendency toward autocratic/authoritarian attitudes, heavy-handed discipline, or lecturing/nagging approaches to "teaching" by the time their child is an adolescent, it will be critical that they make the transition to a more Discipleship Parenting-based approach as soon as possible to avoid the above dangers.

Just like well-regulated children at every other stage of development, it is normal for healthy teens to work to gain their parents' approval, to seek out and respect their parents' advice, and to want to spend time with their parents. Of course, a primary task of adolescence is cultivating meaningful relationships with peers and the world, but when both the teen and the parent-teen relationship are healthy, any potential conflicts between family and peer obligations are simply something to negotiate, not a constant source of tension.

Most of the undesirable and destructive behavior teens get into is a direct result of the adolescent's belief that their parents are either unable, uninterested, or incapable of helping them meet their needs. "Because I said so" approaches to parenting teens favor preserving the illusion of parental authority over the ability of the parent to actually influence their child. The famous baseball coach Yogi Berra, known almost as much for his malapropisms as for his baseball career, once said of his players after a particularly dismal performance, "I taught good. They just learned bad." It's hard to think of a better way to summarize both the attitude and fruit of "because I said so" approaches to raising teenagers.

None of this is to suggest that parents of teens do not have rightful authority over their children. Of course you do! But, like Christ's own authority (see Jn 13:1–17), healthy parental authority is exercised through loving service. Discipleship Parents know that the key to maintaining their authority and influence over their teens is adopting an approach that says, "I'm committed to putting in the time and energy it takes to really understand your needs, teach you how to meet them in a godly ways, and help you figure out how to lead a successful, fulfilling life. Let's do this together!" This is the attitude that fosters secure parent-teen attachment and allows parents to disciple their adolescents into a healthy, godly adulthood.

Maintaining Attachment with Teens

In addition to the above attachment-friendly attitude, all of the habits we suggested for maintaining attachment in the preteen years (such as strong family rituals, the qualified yes technique, and attentive listening skills) apply to adolescence — only more so. In addition, we also recommend maintaining a degree of flexibility that strikes the balance between creating a structure that guides your teens' healthy development and allowing them the freedom to spread their wings and learn to fly on the straight and narrow under their own power. If you did not read the last chapter on the preteen years, particularly the section on maintaining attachment, please take a minute to review those pages now. Properly applying the following advice depends a great deal on the information you will find there.

Strong Family Rituals

Contrary to conventional wisdom, assuming a well-regulated child and a healthy parent-child relationship, teens both appreciate and thrive in households with strong family rituals for working, playing, talking, and praying together. There are several reasons for this. First, family rituals provide a secure base for launching into the world. Family rituals also provide an apprenticeship in healthy "adulting." Finally, family rituals facilitate a strong sense of personal identity. We will cover each of these reasons in more depth in the following sections.

1. Secure Base

Strong family rituals provide teens with a secure base from which to launch. In toddlerhood, the only thing little ones like more than exploring their environment is looking back to see whether you're still there watching them and keeping them safe. Children of all ages exercise their independence more confidently and responsibly when they are given ways to stay connected to the people who love and support them. Strong family rituals for working, playing, talking, and praying help teens remember who they are and to whom they belong. This allows them to create meaningful relationships with peers without losing their sense of identity. Parents often fear the influence peers and "the world" have over their children, as if these things were magical constructs seeking to steal their children away from them. The good news is that peers and society have no innate power to do any such thing. Peers, media, and other outside influences gain power over teens when teens participate in a greater number of rituals outside the home than inside the home, and when those rituals they create with friends, teams, and even media are both more consistent and more compelling than the rituals they participate in at home. The answer isn't to never let your kids leave the house. The answer is to give them consistent and compelling work, play, talk, and prayer rituals that make them want to come home again.

That said, the flexibility we mentioned above is important. Teens need time with peers, and they need time to engage in activities (organized and otherwise) that allow them to build skills and talents and find their place in the world. Forbidding a teen to see friends because they must be at family dinner at six o'clock sharp every night is the quickest way to alienate a teen and undermine the benefits of a family ritual. A better approach is to say, "Having family dinner is important. How can we negotiate dinnertime so that you can still see your friends?" The same would be true for other important family rituals. Except when there is not another option, don't excuse teens from family rituals, but do be willing to make reasonable accommodations whenever possible to allow your teens to maintain their connection to your family and still fulfill their social needs.

2. Apprenticeship in Healthy "Adulting"

"Adulting" refers to the confidence a young person has in their ability to do the things grown-ups do. Although it usually refers to tasks such as paying bills, keeping house, maintaining cars, etc., it also refers to more personal and relational tasks such as keeping schedules, managing priorities, planning activities, and having healthy relationship habits. The ability to successfully "adult" comes from spending time with one's parents, learning to do these things. Rituals facilitate this.

In our experience, one of the most common reasons so many young adults struggle to "adult" successfully is that they did not participate in strong family rituals growing up. They did not have the opportunity to learn to "adult" by witnessing their parents do anything up close. Assuming your household has strong rituals for working, playing, talking, and praying together, as your children become teens, they should be given more and more opportunities to be active partners in facilitating those rituals or even taking charge of those rituals. Family work rituals teach teens creative approaches (as opposed to begrudging approaches) to cooking, cleaning, and maintaining a home. Family play rituals (including holiday traditions as well as more common activities like game nights and family days) teach teens to generate fun ideas for activities, motivate others, and organize events. Family talk rituals teach teens how to express themselves, share their needs, negotiate, empathize, and invest in others. Family prayer rituals help teens learn to reflect and process the events of their day, seek deeper meaning, cultivate their moral sensibilities, and foster a meaningful faith life.

One of the primary tasks of adolescence is facilitating a sense of adult competence. Teens want to feel like they know how to do things and have the skills they need to take care of themselves. Strong family rituals allow you to meet this need in a gentle, non-intrusive manner. As children become more competent participants in family rituals, encourage them to play a more and more active role in facilitating and taking point in maintaining those activities. Let the rituals your family establishes for working, playing, talking, and praying together serve as an apprenticeship program in healthy adulting.

3. Personal Identity

Strong family rituals facilitate a strong sense of personal identity. Research shows that, more than conversation and lectures, rituals convey values, beliefs, and a personal worldview.[1] Rituals teach implicit lessons about priorities, how to make good decisions about what we spend our time and energy on, healthy versus unhealthy ways to connect with others, and what is truly important.

Another major challenge of adolescence is solidifying a healthy sense of identity. Who am I? What do I believe in? What do I stand for? What commitments and relationships are most important? Rituals connect us to our family, our culture, and our faith. They remind us of who we are, to whom we belong, what we stand for, and where we are going. We can either give our teens rituals that connect them to their family, their culture, and their faith, or we can allow them to create their own — largely unconscious — rituals with friends, activities, and media that leave them awash in confusing and conflicting messages about what it means to be a successful human person. By creating compelling family rituals that are simultaneously flexible enough to accommodate your teen's other obligations, you show your teens how they can carry their family's values and priorities into their futures.

The Qualified Yes Technique

We discussed the basic outline of this technique in our chapter on pre-adolescence. Rather than repeat the underlying basis for the technique, we wanted to focus on how the technique could be used for more serious issues related to the mid to later teen years.

Recall that that technique seeks to prevent you, the parent, from setting up an unnecessarily adversarial dynamic with your teen. Obviously, there are times we need to say no unequivocally, and you should never hesitate to do so for matters that you genuinely believe present a clear threat to your teen's physical, emotional, moral, relational, or spiritual health. But for every other request, the qualified yes technique allows you to find a responsible middle ground between being an arbitrary naysayer and being overly permissive.

For instance, if your teen wanted to go on an expensive trip with his school, but you couldn't afford it, rather than saying, "No, we can't afford it," you might say, "I really want you to have that opportunity, but we can only afford to give you X amount toward the cost. I can promise you that amount, but let's work together to see if we can come up with a plan for you to get the rest. What are some of your ideas?"

Let's look at two other examples where the qualified yes technique is particularly useful: driving and dating.

Imagine that your teen is of legal age to get her driving permit. All her friends are studying for the test, but you have serious concerns about her maturity and responsibility. When she asks whether she can start studying for her permit, you might say, "I'm really looking forward to having you be able to take the car out by yourself. It would be a real help to the family to know that I could count on you to run errands for me as well as it just being fun for you to be able to go out by yourself. I want to make sure that you have everything it takes to enjoy that privilege without hurting yourself. In order to know that, I would need to see you paying closer attention to things that need to be done around the house and showing more emotional control when your brother irritates you. I need to be able to count on you showing responsibility and self-control when I can see you before I can completely trust that you can be responsible and have good self-control behind the wheel when I can't be there. Let's make a plan to work on that for the next four weeks. If you can show me by the end of the month that you are remembering to do your chores without being asked, really paying attention to what's happening around you at home, and working harder to deal with your brother respectfully when he is irritating you, I will go with you to the DMV. We'll have a brief chat about your progress every week. If you're having a hard time with it, we may go longer than a month, but that's up to you. What do you say? Are you willing to work with me to get your permit?"

Your teen might respond, "But none of my friends have to do that!" You can easily reply, "I don't really know how much responsibility or self-control your friends have, but I would hope that their parents love them enough that if they didn't have the amount of self-control and responsibility they needed to manage a car well, that they would take a similar approach. I want you to grow up to be successful and have everything you want in life, but I will never let you have a privilege that I think you could hurt yourself with. It's not enough to give you privileges. I want you to be able to enjoy them confidently."

Assuming you take this approach, you would have to commit to regular conversations about what your daughter could do to prove to you that she was showing the self-control and responsibility she needed to succeed in your eyes. You would want to catch her being good when she was doing well and use virtue-prompting when she was struggling. The point is not to make her prove herself to you, but to create a relationship where you are her success coach and she is your student. She needs to do the work, but she knows that she is doing it with your love and support.

This approach facilitates attachment by preventing you from being seen as an insurmountable obstacle for your teen to wear down or overcome. She may roll her eyes at your "ridiculous standards," but your attitude and commitment to help her succeed will show her that your standards are rooted in love and not a petty devotion to an inflated, arbitrary sense of authority.

You can use a similar approach with dating. We'll discuss this topic a bit more in a later section of this chapter, but for the purposes of this example, imagine that your son likes a girl and would like to go on a one-on-one date. (Note: We are specifically avoiding naming an age because dating privileges should be based on emotional and spiritual maturity.) He and the girl have been out together with friends, and he has had her to your house a few times. You don't have any issues with the girl or even with their friendship, but you want to make sure that your son knows how to be a true Christian gentleman when he goes out.

You might say, "I would really like to know that you are ready to handle yourself well on a date, and I think it's great that you want to take Jennifer out, but there are a couple of things that I need to see you do before you can really handle yourself well. First, because being one-on-one with a girl means that you are taking greater responsibility for your moral life, I need to see you doing more to own your spiritual life at home. Let's do a better job of making sure that you're getting some individual prayer time every day, and that you're doing more to lead family prayer. Second, caring about someone doesn't just mean having warm feelings for them; it means that you're committed to serving them and helping them be a better person. Let's talk about some ways you can show me that you're mature enough to do more to work for the good of the people in this house. I really want to see you putting others before yourself because that's what it takes to have a truly healthy, godly relationship. If you can work on that with me for the next couple of weeks, and you do really well, I would be happy to arrange some time for you to go on a date with Jennifer."

Again, you aren't saying no. You are granting permission, but you are setting up the parameters that would increase the likelihood of your son learning what he needs to know to handle a dating relationship well. Obviously this would not be a one-time thing. Rather, this step would represent the first part of a much longer discipleship relationship in which you and your son would regularly and prayerfully explore the virtues and qualities he would need to have a fulfilling, godly relationship with a girl.

The point of the qualified yes technique is to foster discipleship by demonstrating a healthy flexibility that preserves your relationship with your child while not throwing your concerns or authority under the bus. Rather than saying yes or no to your teens' requests, use the qualified yes technique to say, "I think that would be wonderful. Let's look at what you would need to succeed, and let's work together to help you get it."

Active Listening

Everything we already said about this in the preteen chapter stands here as well. The suggestions for active listening with preteens become even more important with adolescents. Teens need to feel heard and understood. They need to know that you are willing to put in the time and energy to really listen before they are willing to accept your advice. That isn't a challenge to your authority. It is a product of their growing independence. God designed teens to start separating from Mom and Dad. Part of that process involves evaluating what to take with them and what to leave behind. Your teens need you to listen to them before offering your thoughts or advice — not because they don't respect your authority, but because they are doing the hard work of trying to fit your teachings into their actual life. If you don't take the time to really hear them and help them see how to apply the lessons you are trying to convey to their actual life, they will struggle to see the relevance of what you are saying. Using the active listening strategies and resources we recommended in the last chapter will help strengthen your attachment to your teen, which will make it more likely that your teen will really absorb whatever guidance you do have to offer.

That said, we wanted to take a moment to emphasize the importance of staying calm in conversations with your teen. Teens have a way of saying things that can be shocking, or saying things in a way that can be upsetting. They can also bring up topics that you might not be ready to address at times you weren't expecting to address them. Our natural reaction is to either get upset, correct them, criticize them, accuse them of being disrespectful, or become outraged, shocked, appalled, or flabbergasted that our teens would say such a thing, think such a thing, or say those things that way. You must resist this temptation with all your might. Make no mistake. Regardless of the good intentions that drive it, this reaction is a temptation that Satan uses to drive a wedge between you and your teen.

Your job — and it's critical — is to do your level best to refrain from ever acting shocked, appalled, or, worst of all, scandalized. Many parents make the mistake of thinking, "If I just react strongly enough to X, my teen will see what a bad idea this is." That might be your intention, but the message your teen gets is, "Mom/Dad can't handle these conversations. They're in over their head. They have nothing useful to say to me. I should go ask someone else what to do." The more emotional you are in response to your teen's questions, requests, or even awkwardly/poorly expressed feelings and opinions, the more you will literally drive your teen away from you, undermine your authority, and all but insist that they listen to … anyone but you.

How can you maintain your cool? Get in the habit of intentionally pausing, even for a second, before responding to anything your teen says that provokes any kind of elevated reaction from you. Taking even a one-second pause before you speak allows your thinking brain to catch up with your emotional brain and increases the likelihood that you will respond well.

Another simple way to allow your brain to catch up is to say, "Wait a second. I got most of that, but you kind of surprised me (with your tone/ with the question/with your request). Say it again so I can make sure I really heard you." This approach has a twofold benefit. It gives you time to calm down and think about your response, and it gives your teen an opportunity to really think about what they want to say and how they want to say it.

Active listening strategies in general, and the ones that allow you to keep your cool in particular, enable you to be flexible enough to really hear what your teen is saying and to respond rather than react.

By committing to strong family rituals, the qualified yes technique, and active listening, you can preserve the attachment you have built with your child through the previous stages of development.

Fostering Emotional Maturity

Adolescence is a notoriously angsty time. Fortunately, if you have been using the techniques we recommended in the section on helping preteens develop emotional regulation, you will be well on the way to teaching your teens to manage their feelings more effectively. Please be sure to read that section before continuing. All of those suggestions will apply here as well. In this chapter, we want to address the challenge of managing the emotional toll hormones can take as well as some additional tips to help teens manage feelings.

Hormones

Teens are experiencing tremendous changes in their bodies as they develop secondary sex characteristics (body hair, chest development, etc.). These physical changes are often accompanied by emotional surges that can be difficult for teens to manage well. Rather than punishing teens for their struggles to manage anger, frustration, sadness, or anxiety, it will be important to teach them how to manage their feelings.

The most important thing to do is to teach your teens the emotional temperature exercise we discussed in the last chapter. Just as physical illness, tiredness, and exhaustion can impact your teen's emotional temperature, hormonal fluctuations can as well. Encourage them to take their emotional temperature throughout the day (breakfast, lunch, dinner, and evening), basing the number not on how they feel, but on the behaviors associated with each number. Having identified their emotional temperature, help them develop the habit of asking themselves, "What is one small thing I could do right now to lower my temperature by at least one point?" Some simple techniques include slowing their speech or actions, praying, seeking appropriate affection from a parent or sibling, taking several deep breaths, or any number of activities your teen can list for themselves. The point is, even though your teen can't control his or her hormones — or any other physical/environmental factors that may be impacting their emotions — your teen can learn to take conscious control of how intensely his or her feelings are impacted by those factors.

Don't make excuses for your teen's surliness or temper, but do treat such displays as an example of your teen's struggle to self-regulate. Don't engage the content of what they say. That will simply result in an unhelpful escalation. Simply empathize with the emotion, then redirect the teen to what they can do about it. For instance, "I understand that you are feeling agitated right now, and I'm sorry you're feeling off. What do you think you need to do to get a better handle on how you're feeling so that you can treat me (all of us) more respectfully?" If your teen isn't cooperative with this approach, you may suggest praying together about the feeling, or, if that fails, that your teen take time to themselves until they can get better regulated. If you do have to ask your teen to take alone time to calm down, don't make a habit of letting them out of their normal responsibilities/chores. Let them know that they will still need to do what is expected of them, but you can't allow them to start until they can treat everyone around them acceptably well. They are in charge of how long it takes to get themselves to that place.

What Feelings Mean

It will also be important to teach your teen that feelings aren't facts. God gave us all of our feelings, but because the world is broken, our emotions don't always work the way God intended them to. The most important question anyone can ask in the face of a feeling is, "Is this feeling helping me respond well to the problem I am facing?" If it is, then that is probably a healthy emotional reaction. If not, my job is to take some time to focus first on calming myself down, rather than trying to do anything about the situation that provoked my emotional reaction.

An emotionally healthy person knows that the first step to getting a handle on a problem is getting a handle on themselves. That doesn't mean stuffing one's emotional reactions. It means taking time to process the feelings. When we are facing any kind of difficulty, we should pray about our feelings, asking God to help us see the problem from other perspectives besides our own — not to dismiss our concerns, but to help us respond better. We should also ask God to help us understand what we are really upset about and how he would like us to respond to the problem in a manner that allows us to glorify him, work for the good of the people involved, and be our best selves. If we're not sure how to do that, we should seek advice from the people who love us and/or know more than we do. Only when we are relatively confident that we have gotten to a place where we are calm can we be sensitive to the concerns of others, and have at least the basic outline of a plan to address the situation that provoked our feelings in the first place. This can take time, but it's worth it. Teach your teen that feelings are not a call to action, but rather, a call to prayer and reflection with an eye toward making a plan.

The approach we outlined above is a simplified version of the approach our team uses at CatholicCounselors.com with teens who are struggling with depression, anxiety, and other emotional problems. This approach not only treats emotional problems but, used properly, can also do a great deal to prevent them.

Fostering Identity

Just as the middle school and preteen years are concerned with developing "industry" (i.e., stick-to-it-iveness), adolescence is the time when teens begin fostering a stronger sense of personal identity. Broadly speaking, having a strong identity involves knowing the answers to four questions:

1. What do I stand for?
2. To whom do I belong?
3. What am I committed to?
4. What can I contribute?

Helping your teen develop a personal mission statement is an excellent way to help them answer these questions.

Personal Mission Statement

Teens are passionate, but they sometime struggle with knowing what they should be passionate about. Teens are very aware of injustices in the world, but they need help figuring out the best way to respond to those problems. Parents often struggle with lecturing their teens in their attempts to guide their developing social consciences. A better approach is to help your teens develop a personal mission statement. This simple exercise is a terrific way to help your teens grow personally and discern the best way to spend their energy. Earlier, we discussed how to develop a family mission statement. The process is similar here. The goal is to first help the teen reflect on the qualities God is calling them to exemplify in their life. Next, you will ask your teen to reflect on the behaviors and choices that would allow them to live out these qualities in their everyday life. Finally, you will help your teen use their mission statement to choose activities and other outlets that help them get involved and make a positive difference in their world.

Personal mission statements are tremendous tools for teen discipline. Teens hate hypocrites. You can use this to your advantage. For instance, if your teen has indicated that he wants to be "responsible" on his mission statement, but he isn't following through on his chores, rather than punishing or lecturing, your first response should be to say, "I know you said that being seen as a responsible person is important to you. Can you help me understand how your attitude toward your chores is reflecting that?" Or if your teen says that she wants to be known as a caring person, but she is being selfish and disrespectful, you might say, "I know that being thought of as a caring person is important to you. Do you think you could talk to me about your concerns in a way that shows me you care about me too? Because right now, that isn't coming across at all." The point isn't to scold or lecture. It is to simply hold up a mirror to help your teen learn to compare their behavior against the values they claim are important to them.

Don't try to develop your teen's mission all at once. Take your time. It's best to do this over several one-on-one outings where you have time to talk, not just about this, but also about other things that are important to your teen as well. Do your best to let this exercise evolve out of these conversations. Here are some simple questions you can ask to help your teen develop a healthy personal mission statement:

> a. What are the qualities, strengths, or values that you think would help you be your best self and live your best life?

Chances are, you have a word or two that come to mind when you think of certain friends. "He's the athletic one." "She's really artistic." "He really studies hard." The fact is, all the people we know have one or two words that come to mind when they think about us too. Those words are the message our life sends to the people around us. God wants our lives to send messages to others that inspire them to love him. As Christians, it's our job to ask God what message he wants our lives to send to others. The best way to do that is to prayerfully consider the qualities, virtues, or strengths that you feel most strongly about. Here is a partial list. Feel free to choose from among these or list other qualities, strengths, or values that you think would help you be your best self and live your best life.

Godly	Loving	Hopeful
Courageous	Balanced	Persistent
Just	Responsible	Generous
Peaceful	Kind	Wise
Patient	Gentle	Modest

Joyful	Self-controlled	Strong
Creative	Faithful	Helpful
Reliable	Supportive	

What other qualities do you think would help you be your best self and live your best life? Write them here.

b. Write down a few examples of common challenges you face in your day. If you were to apply the above strengths to those challenges, how might you respond differently than you usually do?

_____

_____

_____

c. Is there something you would need to do or change about the way you live, the choices you make, or the way you spend your time in order for others to think of these qualities when they think of you?

_____

_____

_____

d. What people or groups do the most to help you live out these qualities in your everyday life? What people or groups tend to make it hard for you to live out these qualities?

_____

_____

e. What social or charitable causes give you the best chance to use these strengths to make a positive difference in your world? What opportunities do you have to become more involved in these causes?

_____

_____

_____

This is a simple version of a personal mission statement. An excellent resource for developing this further is *The 7 Habits of Highly Effective Teens* by Sean Covey.

Fostering Faith Development

The following section will offer some highlights for addressing faith development in the teen years. For more comprehensive advice, please see our book *Discovering God Together: The Catholic Guide to Raising Faithful Kids.*

Research by psychologist James Fowler suggests that faith evolves in different stages. Teens fall into what we call the "relationship stage" of faith development. Generally speaking, teens believe that something is true to the degree that it helps them facilitate meaningful relationships, and something is false to the degree that it makes having meaningful relationships more difficult. Although there are several adult faith stages, many people never evolve out of the relationship stage of faith development (which Fowler called the "synthetic conventional stage").

The fact that teens' faith is relational means that, to increase the likelihood they will raise faithful teens, parents must:

1. Help their teens foster a personal and emotional relationship with Christ
2. Help their teens see how their faith is making a difference and how their faith can help their teens make a difference
3. Help their teens see how their faith can help them create

meaningful relationships and provide clarity in the face of relationship drama

1. Help teens foster a personal and emotional relationship with Christ

First, it is critical that parents do what they can to help their teens foster a personal and emotional relationship with God. Children in the story and structure stage of faith development (middle childhood/preteen) were content to learn to say prayers and engage in spiritual habits. While these behaviors can serve as the foundation to a relationship with God, they do not necessarily lead to a relationship with God. Although some younger children can and do make a personal connection with God, for the most part, most children are happy that doing these things makes them feel grown up and makes their parents happy. But when children reach adolescence, they need to know *why* they are doing the things they are doing, and they need to know for whom they are doing them. If parents have not helped their children relate to God as an actual person who knows them best and loves them most, teens will come to dismiss their former pious practices as empty words and actions. This may be one of the reasons research shows that many Catholic children who lose their faith do so between ages eleven and thirteen.

Parents need to speak of God using personal language. We need to share with our teens how we see God impacting our life. Teens need to see that God makes a real difference in the lives of those around them. It isn't enough that we tell them about God. We need to show them that being in relationship with him makes a positive difference in our lives. We need to talk about that difference. Meaningful talk rituals such as family meals, family meetings, and one-on-one time give us the opportunity to have these kinds of conversations.

It's also important to lead our teens in more emotional/relational approaches to prayer (for instance, praise and worship music, charismatic prayer, and praying from the heart). These prayer forms and practices help teens feel God's presence tangibly and concretely. Because teens' faith is relational, they need to feel God's presence to know he is real. When teens say, "I don't believe in God," the most common reason is that they haven't experienced his presence in any meaningful way. There are other factors we discuss in *Discovering God Together,* but for most teens, saying, "I don't believe in God" means, "I've been saying words at God for a long time, but I've never experienced him saying anything back or wanting to connect with me in any real way." It can be very helpful if you are fortunate enough to be in an area that has a dynamic youth group that engages in more emotional approaches to prayer; but even if not, you should also be doing praise and worship and more emotional/personal/relational types of prayer *at home.* Any spiritual development that happens outside your home should support what you are already doing at home, rather than making up for what is missing at home. Take part in showing your teen that God really cares about him or her personally by teaching them to pray from the heart and to hear God speaking to their heart.

Teaching our teens how to listen to God in prayer is an incredibly important part of teaching them that God is real. Without these skills, teens experience prayer as "saying words at God" instead of an actual relationship with God. Help your teen use the PRAISE format we discussed earlier. Give them time before family prayer to walk through the PRAISE format on their own. In fact, it is a good habit for your whole family to take at least ten to fifteen minutes or more per evening to pray individually before gathering as a family. Make part of your family prayer time discussing how God is speaking to your hearts.

If you feel a little intimidated by the idea of teaching your teens to listen to God speaking to them in prayer, don't be. Many parents struggle to hear God speaking to them. Although, on rare occasions, God does make it abundantly clear that he is speaking to us, for the most part he "speaks" by inclining our hearts and minds in one direction or another as we pray, gather information, and pray some more. Because his voice is subtle, we can get confused. We worry, "How do I know this is God's voice and not my own?" Saint Ignatius of Loyola offers a few tests to make sure that we are hearing God clearly and correctly when we pray.

First, God will never ask us to do something that contradicts his commandments or the teachings of the Church. The commandments and the doctrines of the Church represent beliefs that have emerged out of thousands of years of conversations between God and all the believers who have ever lived. It isn't that God won't tell us to do something that is contrary to the commandments or the teachings of the Church because "those are the rules." It's because all the Christians who make up the Church since the very beginning have been having a prayerful conversation with God about what it means to live a happy, holy, healthy life. The commandments and doctrines of the Church represent the things God has taught us through thousands of years of prayerful reflection about what it means to be a healthy, happy, fully human person. God isn't going to contradict the conversation he's been having over thousands of years with billions of people to say, "But on the other hand, now that I think about it, Bob really is the exception."

Second, the Holy Spirit is always going to nudge us toward choices and actions that help us draw closer to God and become the person God wants us to be. And who does God want us to be? People who pursue meaningfulness, intimacy, and virtue.

He wants us to be people who live meaningful lives by using our gifts and talents to benefit us and bless others. He wants us to build his kingdom by always working to make our relationships with others deeper, healthier, and stronger. And he wants us to pursue virtue by treating all the things that life throws at us as opportunities to become stronger, healthier, godlier people. Saint Ignatius called any impulse, feeling, thought, or desire that pushes us toward these goals a "consolation." A consolation is the voice of the Holy Spirit. It doesn't matter if it "sounds" like the Holy Spirit's voice or not. It might sound like our voice, or the voice of a friend, or even the voice of someone on TV. It might not be a voice at all. Perhaps it's just a feeling or an inclination. It doesn't matter. If that "movement of the Spirit" (to use Saint Ignatius's phrase) points us toward those goals, it is actually God's voice speaking to us and telling us to go in that direction.

By contrast, any thought, feeling, desire, or impulse that points us in the opposite direction — toward powerlessness, isolation, or self-pity and self-indulgence — is really the voice of the Enemy trying to pull us away from God. Saint Ignatius called these impulses "desolations." When we pray about our daily life, our job is to reject desolations and ask, "What would the Holy Spirit have me do? How could I respond to this in a way that would help me use my gifts and talents to be effective and bless others, make my relationships stronger and healthier, and use what life is throwing at me to be a stronger, healthier, godlier person?" The more I pray this way, the more I learn to hear God speaking to me as a real person who knows me best and loves me most.

2. Help teens see how their faith is making a difference and how their faith can help them make a difference
Research shows that if parents want to pass their faith on to their kids, they need to be able to share simple stories about how God is making a difference in their daily lives.[2] Our teens need to hear us praising God for the little blessings that occur throughout the day, asking for God's help with the various challenges we face, and praising him for answered prayers.

Building on this, we need to help our teens do the same. When they come to us with a problem, we should first empathize with them. They need to feel that we are giving them our time, attention, and hearts. But before we give any advice, we should help them pray about this situation in their own words and ask them what they think God is saying to them. When good things happen, in addition to celebrating with them, we should help them praise God in their own words for those blessings. Teach your teens to see God moving in their lives in powerful ways.

Teens naturally want to make a difference. Teach your teen how their faith can help them maximize their potential to have a positive impact on the world. Help your teen pray about how they can use their God-given gifts and talents to work for the good of their family, their community, and the world at large. Talk with them about the people and causes they feel the most concern for. Together, learn what the Church teaches about responding to these concerns. Discuss any differences that might exist between the world's approaches to these problems and the Church's approach. Look for opportunities for them to get involved in faithful groups that advocate for these causes or serve these people. Too often, teens come to think of their Christian faith as a list of rules that tells people what not to do, but offers no answers for real problems. Show them this isn't the case. Help them see that being a Christian is about finding godly, practical, concrete answers to the problems sin has inflicted on the world.

3. Help teens see how their faith can help them create meaningful relationships and provide clarity in the face of relationship drama

Recall that teens generally believe that anything that complicates relationships tends to be false, while anything that facilitates relationships tends to be true. Many teens lose their faith when parents blame their Catholicism for not allowing them to associate with certain people or engage in certain activities. Help your teens see how their faith can help them have a more meaningful, peaceful, drama-free social life.

Many parents think that signing up their teen for youth group will check this box. It may certainly help (if it is truly a good and faithful group with good and faithful kids), but don't think that's where your job ends.

Earlier, we discussed the importance of helping your teen develop a personal mission statement. This exercise can help you provide guidance about your teens' relationships without resorting to lecturing. Teens often struggle to know the difference between healthy and unhealthy relationships. The answer is that healthy relationships make me want to work harder to live out my mission, while unhealthy relationships make it harder to live out my mission. When you have concerns about your teen's relationships, don't lead with, "I don't like you hanging out with so-and-so." Start with something like, "I really like that you are friends with lots of different and interesting people, but when I hear you talking about (Name), I wonder how he/she is affecting your ability to live out your mission. Can you tell me more about that?"

Teach your teen to use their mission statement to evaluate the health of their various relationships. If your teen tries to put it on you, saying something like, "You're trying to tell me who I can be friends with!" simply say, "I am not doing that at all. You told me that being X kind of person is important to you, and the only thing that's important to me is helping you be the person you say you want to be. I'm just asking you to help me see how this relationship is helping you be the person you claim you want to be." Keep your opinion out of the conversation as much as possible. Instead, keep asking your teen to justify their actions based on their own mission. As we mentioned earlier, teens hate hypocrisy. Using this approach allows you to convey concerns in a manner that your teen will respect.

Of course, even the healthiest teen relationships are fraught with drama of one kind or another. When your teen is struggling with the latest crisis over "who did/said what to whom," instead of offering your opinion, teach them to think faithfully about their challenges. As always, start by empathizing and expressing how sad/frustrated/disappointed/concerned you are that they have to go through this. Then pray with them. When possible, ask them to lead. Ask God to help the two of you figure out the best way to respond to the challenge and to give your teen the grace to do the best thing even when it's hard. Ask them what they think God would want them to do. Ask them, if they were to apply the qualities they identified in their mission statement, what would their mission tell them to do? If certain issues raise questions that touch on faith and morals, don't lecture your child. Go online and look up reliable sources for what the Church teaches on those matters. Read and discuss it together. Ask your teen how they think this information might impact their choices. Help them experience their faith as a guide to help them negotiate life and relationship drama in a way that is both graceful and helps them hold on to their sense of self.

Fostering Healthy Psycho-Sexual Development

Another important part of fostering teens' identity is facilitating their psycho-sexual development. We will present some highlights here. For readers interested in learning more, we encourage you to check out our book *Beyond the Birds and the Bees.* Likewise, the following recommendations presume that readers are already making use of the ideas listed in the previous chapter on preteens.

Briefly, fostering healthy psycho-sexual development in adolescents involves the following:

1. Helping teens recognize the difference between healthy and unhealthy romantic relationships
2. Helping teens live the Christian vision of love
3. Helping teens understand the role of feelings in romantic relationships
4. Helping teens understand the self-giving language of the body

5.   Polishing the eight virtues at the heart of a healthy sexuality

1. Helping teens recognize the difference between healthy and unhealthy romantic relationships
Many parents approach the question of dating as an age issue. They state an age at which their teens can date and hope that the teen will be mature enough by then. This leaves entirely too much to chance and omits the parent from the role of forming young people who are capable of having godly relationships with members of the opposite sex. Discipleship Parents understand that dating presents a wonderful opportunity to mentor their children in the Christian vision of love. The Christian vision of love is very different from the world's vision. Teens can't learn to live this vision just by being told what to do and not to do. They need people who love them to guide — not lecture — them. That is where the Discipleship Parent comes in.

Just as you used the personal mission statement to help your teen assess healthy and unhealthy friendships, you can use the same exercise to help your teen assess healthy versus unhealthy romantic relationships. When you are in a healthy romantic relationship, your partner's influence and presence makes you want to even more faithfully pursue becoming the person you say you want to be, stand up for the things you claim to believe in, and pursue the goals that are important to you. An unhealthy romantic relationship makes you afraid to assert your opinions or interests for fear of losing the other person. It makes you feel ashamed or awkward about standing up for what you believe in. It makes you feel that pursuing your personal goals is an unwanted distraction from holding on to the relationship at all costs.

The earlier you can convey this information to your teen, the better. If you can discuss this early enough, preferably before your teen's friends start dating, you can help your teen assess their friends' experience through this lens as well as their own. The point is not to judge their friends, but rather to give your teens real-life opportunities to see this principle at work.

In the original edition of *Parenting with Grace*, we shared the story of a young woman who was quite smitten with a boy in her class. The parents had concerns about the young man, but hoped to avoid a direct confrontation. They had already led her through developing a personal mission statement, so they asked her to reflect on those qualities in light of the relationship. Sure, it made her feel good to be around him, but when she was around him, did she feel more courageous to be true to the virtues, beliefs, and goals she listed on her mission statement? Or did she feel like she had to hide these things, be dishonest about these things, or be afraid he would reject her for these things?

All of a sudden, she began to tear up. She said, "This sucks. I *really* like him, but I know he isn't good for me because he really doesn't believe in any of the same things I do. We like to do some of the same stuff, but that's not enough." Rather than trying to lecture her out of this less-than-ideal relationship, this young woman's Discipleship Parents were able to support her decision, praise her maturity, and help her stand up for what she knew was best for her despite her conflicted feelings.

2. Helping teens live the Christian vision of love

We recently asked our fourteen-year-old, "What is the point of being Christian?" The obvious answer is "to follow Christ." But why did he come in the first place? Why do we *need* to follow him? This question led to a very interesting discussion about what many people think makes them Christian versus what actually makes them Christian.

For instance, some people would say that the point of being a Christian is "to have a good life and be protected from problems," but that's foolish. Our faith doesn't prevent us from suffering. It shows us how to respond to suffering in a way that glorifies God, works for the good of the people around us, and helps us become our best selves.

Others might say that the point of being a Christian is to learn "to be a good person," but you can be a good person without following Christ. Lots of atheists do good deeds.

Why are you a Christian? Why is your teen?

The real point of being a Christian is recognizing that only by following Christ can we learn to love the way God wants us to love one another — in a manner that works for the ultimate good of everyone involved. Jesus tells us, "Love one another. As I have loved you. ... This is how all will know that you are my disciples" (Jn 13:34–35). Jesus calls this his "new commandment" because his life illustrates a very different vision of love than the world offers. We cannot call ourselves disciples of Christ unless we consciously reject everything the world tells us about love and learn, instead, to live the love that comes from the Father's heart.

This has a direct impact on your teen's ability to have healthy relationships — especially healthy romantic relationships. Everyone wants to be thought of as a loving person. We all *feel* love in our hearts for people. But it's hard to know how to express that love in ways that are actually *loving*. How often do we see people genuinely trying to be loving, only to end up hurting themselves or others in the process? The world's vision of love is often well intentioned, but it is deeply destructive. Christian disciples are called to show how Christ's love has the power to save us from the trap of destructive "loving."

For instance, the world tells us that love is just a feeling, and that as long as you are being true to your feelings, you are being loving — no matter how many lives are ruined in the process. The Christian vision of love says that — regardless of our feelings — we are not being loving unless the things we do help us and the people we love become our best selves in Christ.

The world says that "love is love," and if a relationship makes me feel good, it is good. The Christian vision of love says that relationships are only good to the degree that they promote the dignity, life, health, and growth of everyone involved.

The world says that love is meant to make *this* life easier. The Christian vision says that true love must bless us in this life *and the next*, and it can only do that through an ongoing commitment to "renunciation, purification, and healing."[3]

To be a disciple of Christ is to be willing to say, "I have a lot of love in my heart, but I don't know how to share it in a way that works for my good and the good of the people I love. That's why I need to give all my relationships to God and ask for his grace every day to help me only be in relationships that allow me to work for my ultimate good and the ultimate good of the people I care about."

To like someone is to have warm feelings for them, but that's not necessarily love.

To desire someone is to be sexually attracted to them, but that's not necessarily love.

To enjoy someone's company is to have affection for them, but that's not necessarily love.

To not be able to get someone out of our minds and hearts is to be obsessed with someone, but that's not necessarily love.

We can have some or all of these feelings for someone without actually loving them. In fact, any time we use any of these feelings as the basis for a relationship instead of true Christian love, we run a very high risk of hurting ourselves or the person we claim to care about.

In contrast to all of the above, true Christian love is committed to always working for both our own ultimate good and the ultimate good of the person we claim to care for. Christian love is *freely given* (not pressured), *total* (not half-hearted or halfway), *faithful* (not just for now), and *fruitful* (encouraging life and well-being). God doesn't want us to settle. He wants us to have relationships — especially romantic relationships — that are founded on true Christian love and include all those other feelings and blessings too. But when we just settle for any or all of those other feelings, without basing our relationship on a commitment to work for each other's ultimate good and build a free, total, faithful, and fruitful life with the person we love, we cheat ourselves out of all the love God wants to give us.

Your teen might ask, "What does working for each other's ultimate good mean?" The short answer is that working for the good of another person involves standing up for their dignity as a son or daughter of God, never doing anything that would jeopardize their life, health, or well-being, and always encouraging their growth (for instance, by actively supporting — and not just tolerating — the kinds of Christ-centered mission statements we spoke of earlier in the book). On top of this, working for the other person's good in a romantic relationship means refusing to settle for anything less than building a free, total, faithful, and fruitful love together. In a truly Christian romantic relationship, everything we say and do for our beloved must communicate the message, "I will love all of you (i.e., I will work for the good of every part of you) always. I will help you become your very best self in Christ, and I will let you help me become my very best self in Christ too. Any relationship — especially any romantic relationship — that doesn't do these things is beneath our dignity as children of God and less than God wants for us.

3. Helping teens understand the role of feelings in romantic relationships

Christians have a conflicted relationship with feelings. On the one hand, we all have them, and they can be awfully hard to ignore. On the other hand, they can get us into a lot of trouble. This is particularly true of romantic feelings.

In 2 Corinthians 10:4–5, Saint Paul says: "We destroy arguments and every pretension raising itself against the knowledge of God, and take every thought captive in obedience to Christ." This is the Christian approach to feelings, and it just so happens that it is completely consistent with a healthy psychology of emotions.

Many people believe that feelings just are. We have them, and they are part of us. This isn't entirely true. Insights from cognitive therapy teach us that feelings can occur spontaneously, but we are only affected by the feelings we choose to hold on to. But why would we hold on to unhealthy feelings? Usually because we don't know other, healthier ways to meet the needs those feelings are trying to serve. For instance, the degree to which I don't know healthy ways to take care of myself or get others to take care of me tends to be directly related to the likelihood that I will struggle to let go of feelings of depression. The degree to which I don't know healthy ways to protect myself from things I perceive as threats is the degree to which I have a hard time letting go of feelings of anxiety. Likewise, the degree to which I lack confidence in my ability to find a person with whom I can have a healthy and godly relationship is the degree to which I will have a hard time letting go of my feelings for a person who is bad for me or doesn't/can't love me back.

We all have these feelings from time to time, and assuming these and other negative emotions aren't ruling our lives, the simplest way to deal with feelings that lead us toward, or keep us trapped in, unhealthy and ungodly relationships is to do what Saint Paul says in 2 Corinthians: bring those feelings to God and ask him to help us meet the needs that are driving those feelings in ways that are pleasing to him and help us become who he wants us to be.

Teach your teens to bring all their feelings to God, especially their romantic feelings. One good way to do this is with a prayer like the following: "Lord, I am feeling X (about this person/situation), and even though I know these feelings are leading me to want (someone/something) that I shouldn't want or can't have, I don't know how to let them go. Show me what you are trying to teach me about myself through these feelings. Help me to discover the needs that are driving these feelings and help me learn to meet them in ways that please you and help me be the person you want me to be. Don't ever let me settle for less than all the love and health and grace you want to give me."

Christians aren't afraid of feelings, even feelings that make us want things (or people) that may not be good for us. Instead of fearing these feelings, repressing them, denying them, or obsessing over them, the Christian is called to "test" these feelings, submitting them to God in prayer and learning how to meet the needs that drive them in godly ways so that we can learn to make every thought and feeling that flows from them "obedient to Christ."

4. Helping teens understand the self-giving language of the body

Christians have a very different understanding of the body than the world does. Essentially, the world tells us that our body belongs to us and we are free to do with it as we choose, especially when it comes to love.

By contrast, Christians understand that our bodies are actually part of the One Body of Christ. Saint Paul says, "Do you not know that your bodies are members of Christ?" (1 Cor 6:15a). Baptized into Christ's family, we are to be his physical presence in the world. When we do anything with our bodies that is beneath our dignity as sons and daughters of God, or when we use our bodies to do things that could hurt ourselves or another person in any way, we deface the image of Christ. What we do with our bodies matters a great deal to God. A little later in that same chapter as the verse we quoted above, Saint Paul goes on to say, "Do you not know that your body is a temple of the holy Spirit within you, whom you have from God, and that you are not your own? For you have been purchased at a price. Therefore, glorify God in your body" (1 Cor 6:19–20).

Many Christians mistakenly think that "God doesn't care what I do with my body, especially in the bedroom. That's private." As long as we think holy thoughts and say our prayers, our body is irrelevant. This is why the Church spends so much time talking about sins against the

Christian vision of love and sex. It isn't because it thinks sex is bad. It's because Christians recognize that our bodies are not ours to do with as we please. Our job is to show the world what it means to be loved by Christ. That doesn't just apply to matters of social justice. It also applies to personal and sexual matters. God wants all boyfriends and girlfriends, and later, each husband and wife, to be a physical sign of how much they are loved by God even more than how much they love each other. We don't ask our teens to abstain from sex before marriage because sex is bad. We ask them to wait for marriage so that they can give everything to each other that a truly healthy, truly passionate, truly holy sexual relationship promises: a free, total, faithful, and life-giving love that lasts a lifetime and fills their hearts with the passion that flows from God's heart (see Song of Songs).

In his Theology of the Body, Saint John Paul taught that God made our bodies not so that we could just pleasure ourselves (in all possible senses of that phrase), but so that we could serve each other, work for each other's good at all times, and be a physical sign of God's love to everyone in our lives.

While many parents assume that having a body is enough to qualify their teen to figure out what to do with it (as long as they lecture their kids on what not to do with it), Discipleship Parents understand the need to teach their children to have a positive relationship with their body. They help their teens learn good hygiene and how to dress in a modest but attractive manner that enables them to be good stewards of the body God gave them and appropriately celebrate the beauty God created in them (see Psalm 139).

Likewise, Discipleship Parents seek to convey a healthy and positive view of sexual morality. God didn't give us bodies so that we could not do certain things with them. He gave us bodies so that we could learn to do all things — especially love one another — in ways that were pleasing to him, ways that work for both our good and the good of those we care about. In this way, everyone who encounters us could know how much they were loved — not just by us, but by God.

Teach your teens that God wants them to have the most passionate love they could imagine in their lives, but that the most passionate way to love someone is to be able to say to them, "I love you so much I would never want to do anything that would make you feel anything less than the love God wants me to give you."

5. Polishing the eight virtues at the heart of a healthy sexuality

Finally, teaching your teens how to have a healthy relationship with love, their body, and sexuality is much more about forming their character in general. The *Catechism* tells us that sexuality reveals the intimate heart of our whole character. Sexual virtue is rooted in a well-formed, strong, godly character. Similarly, sexual problems are not rooted in sex, but rather in weaknesses in a person's overall character.

In our book *Beyond the Birds and the Bees: Raising Sexually Whole and Holy Kids,* we identify eight virtues that exist at the heart of a healthy sexuality. The degree to which your teen exhibits each virtue — not just in dating relationships but in every part of life — points to another source of strength that will feed their healthy, godly, sexual attitudes and behavior. The degree to which your teen struggles to exhibit any of these virtues — not just in dating relationships but in every part of life (especially within your home and in their relationship with you) — is the degree to which you can expect your teen to struggle with problematic sexual attitudes and behavior. Each one of us is a work in progress, and developing all of these virtues is a lifelong project. Even so, the more you can help your teen develop these virtues fully in every area of their life, the more you can feel confident that your teen will be capable of actively working to live out the Christian vision of love and sex.

On a scale of 1 (My teen seriously struggles with this) to 5 (My teen is very strong in this), rate how strong your teen is in each of the following virtues:

___1. Self-Giving Love — The ability, in general, to eagerly and actively work to make the lives of those around them easier and more pleasant through their generous service and caretaking, even when it is hard or inconvenient. Relates to sexuality in that it helps your teen choose to love in ways that are pleasing to God and consistent with their ultimate good and the ultimate good of their beloved.

___2. Responsibility — This includes doing chores without being told but goes far beyond it. It primarily refers, in general, to having the ability to respond in healthy, godly ways (rather than having the tendency to *react* in inappropriate, impulsive ways) to the things that happen to him or her. Relates to sexuality in that it gives teens the ability to control inappropriate expressions of desire and attraction and channel that energy in a healthy, appropriate manner.

___3. Faith — The ability to demonstrate a meaningful, personal relationship with Christ and an active prayer life. In general, helps the teen to know what they are worth in God's eyes and to want to place God's will above their own. Relates to sexuality in that it helps teens to connect to the bigger picture and makes them want to love others with God's love more than their own.

___4. Respect — In general, helps teens understand their own God-given dignity and the God-given dignity of others. Relates to sexuality in that it helps them impose healthy boundaries on others and respect the healthy boundaries of others, even when it is difficult.

___5. Intimacy — In general, helps teens express their needs, feelings, thoughts, desires, and hopes and dreams in a transparent and appropriate manner. Relates to sexuality in that people who struggle with intimacy tend to try to make up for it by overemphasizing the physical aspects of romantic relationships.

___6. Cooperation — In general, helps teens negotiate ways to meet their own needs while respecting the needs of others. This virtue decreases the likelihood of the teen trying to control others or be controlled by others, both in general and in romantic relationships.

___7. Joy — In general, helps the teen celebrate life and know how to pursue pleasure and enjoyment in healthy, godly, life-affirming ways. Relates to sexuality by helping teens see not just "the rules" but also the positive, life-affirming intentions behind healthy sexual morals. Also, some people who struggle to be joyful can be prone to "self-medicating" with sex and other compulsive activities.

___8. Personhood — In general, refers to a teen's ability to have a healthy, positive relationship with his or her body, and a healthy sense of his or her masculinity/femininity. Relates to sexuality in that teens with healthy personhood aren't tempted to prove their masculinity/femininity by playing into sexual stereotypes or sexual precociousness.

If you would like to explore each of these virtues in more depth, we recommend reading *Beyond the Birds and the Bees*, which looks at this process at length as well as offers a comprehensive, developmental perspective on fostering a healthy Christian vision of love in your children. For our purposes here, it's enough to know that most teens' (indeed, most people's) struggles with sexuality have very little to do with sex and everything to do with an underdeveloped relationship with one or more of the above virtues. If your teen is struggling with one or more of these qualities, discuss them as part of building your teen's mission statement and use the suggestions you will find in *Beyond the Birds and the Bees* to strengthen this aspect of their character.

Conclusion

The teenage years are a tremendously exciting time for Discipleship Parents. These are the years you help your teen take all the lessons you have been trying to teach them since they were small children and put it all together so that they can own these values and apply them in ways that help them create a fulfilling, godly life. While these years can be full of challenges, big questions, and bigger drama, it is a privilege to see young men and young women coming into their own and making independent choices that reflect their love for Christ and their desire to please him in all they do. While other people and peers will play a larger role throughout the teen years, Discipleship Parents make sure to invest the time and energy they need to pour into their relationship with their teen so that they can maintain the attachment that gives them the credibility required to form their adolescents into healthy, godly adults. Because these are such important years, resist the temptation to simply write off ongoing breakdowns in your relationship with your teen or dismiss habitual surliness, animosity, or rebelliousness as a "phase." Don't hesitate to seek appropriate pastoral counseling assistance early if problems persist, because any of these dynamics could seriously increase the likelihood that your teens will turn to peers or others for guidance on managing the challenges of adolescence. Peers and others only have the power we give them by neglecting the quality of our own discipleship relationship with our teens.

The good news is that the more you are able to foster the healthy attachment that stands at the heart of Discipleship Parenting, the more you will see your teen actively seeking your advice and guidance in ways that may surprise you. As you guide them, be sure to let your heavenly Father minister to you, healing your own teen wounds and helping you grow in love, confidence, and gratitude for the privilege you have been given in shaping the next generation of healthy, dynamic Christian disciples.

Prayer

Lord, help me be a good mentor to my teen. Help me to see these years as an opportunity to prepare them to become healthy, fulfilled, godly adults. Give me the grace to not live in fear of the challenges I will face, but to embrace them as an opportunity to grow closer together. Help me to accompany my teen through these years and be the mentor and model they need to discover your plan for living a joyful, love-filled life.

Discussion Questions

How is God using your relationship with your teen to help you draw closer to him?

What ideas did you find most useful in this chapter? What ideas challenged you?

How will you use the things you learned in this chapter to strengthen your relationship with your teen?

CONCLUSION

Living the Liturgy of Domestic Church Life

In the Eucharist the sacrifice of Christ becomes also
the sacrifice of the members of his Body. The lives
of the faithful, their praise, sufferings, prayer, and
work, are united with those of Christ and with his
total offering, and so acquire a new value.

CCC 1368

Thank you for allowing us to accompany you on this part of your parenting journey. We hope you can see what a radically different, radically faithful system Discipleship Parenting is. The most important takeaway from this book is that, for Catholics especially, parenting isn't just about parenting. It is, ultimately, a spiritual exercise — a participation in the celebration of what could be called the Liturgy of Domestic Church Life. We first introduced this idea back in chapter 3. We'd like to offer some final suggestions for celebrating this liturgy in full and unlocking the spiritual potential of your family.

Celebrating the Liturgy of Domestic Church Life

Recall how we said that liturgy is the work God does through the Church to heal the damage that sin does to our relationships with him and others. In the Liturgy of the Eucharist, God restores our union with him and makes communion with others possible. By extension, the Liturgy of Domestic Church Life allows us to bring Jesus home and make our faith the source of the warmth in our home. Through the Liturgy of Domestic Church Life, our broken, sinful, struggling families are consecrated to Christ and equipped to become something sacred and divine: dynamic domestic churches! As a domestic church, the Holy Spirit enables you to fill your home with Christ's love, allows every aspect of family life to be filled with God's grace, and ultimately empowers you to consecrate the world to Christ. (If you're interested in understanding the theological basis for this Liturgy of Domestic Church Life, we recommend that you read *Renewing Catholic Family Life*, the book produced following the Symposium on Catholic Family Life and Spirituality in 2019.

Getting Family Life "Rite"

All the "stuff" Discipleship Parents do all day is not just spiritual, it's *liturgical*. That is to say, it's meant to help parents do our part to cooperate with God's grace and heal the damage sin has done to our human relationships — especially in our homes. Everything we do all day is ministry, if we do it with the intention of communicating God's love to our spouse and kids.

That said, every liturgy is composed of various rites. Rites are, in a sense, the building blocks of liturgy. For instance, the Liturgy of the Eucharist has an opening rite, a penitential rite, an offertory rite, a Communion rite, and a concluding rite, just to name a few. These rites guide us through a meaningful celebration of the Eucharist. The absence of any of these rites could negatively impact the quality, integrity, or even validity of the Mass.

Although we haven't categorized them in this way before now, most of this book has actually been describing the three rites of the Liturgy of Domestic Church Life. They are the Rite of Christian Relationship, the Rite of Family Rituals, and the Rite of Reaching Out. Each of these rites helps parents and kids live out different aspects of their baptismal missions to be priests, prophets, and royals.

- *The Rite of Christian Relationship:* A priest's job is to offer sacrifices that make things holy and build a bridge between heaven and earth. Godly families live out the priestly mission of their baptism by loving one another, not just with the love that comes naturally to us as broken, sinful people, but with sacrificial, Christian love. When Christian families intentionally make little sacrifices to work for one another's good throughout the day, we consecrate our homes to Christ, help each other become holy, and make our homes a sacred space. Our common, messy, crazy households become domestic churches.

- *The Rite of Family Rituals:* A prophet is someone who reminds God's people how they are meant to live. When we make a little time to work, play, talk, and pray together every day, we model how Christians are meant to relate to work, leisure, relationships, and faith, and we witness to the world how Christians are called to live. This is the main way parents and kids can help one another practice the prophetic mission of our baptism.

- *The Rite of Reaching Out:* To serve with Christ is to reign with him. As Christians, we're meant to be a blessing to others. When we go about our day keeping others in mind, being kind, charitable, hospitable, serving others, and discerning our family mission and charisms, we serve with Christ and build the kingdom of God. Practicing the Rite of Reaching Out is the main way parents and kids help one another practice the royal mission of our baptism.

Each of these rites contributes something important to your domestic church's ability to be happy and healthy, and to experience every part (even the messy parts) of family life as sacred. By understanding how the various practices we've described in *Parenting with Grace* fit into the three rites of the Liturgy of Domestic Church Life, you can see how every part of your parenting life is meant to be a prayer. Let's pull it all together and briefly look at how you can experience the Faith as the source of the warmth in your home by practicing each of the three rites of the Liturgy of Domestic Church Life.

Liturgy of Domestic Church Life Quiz

The following quiz can help summarize the different practices associated with the Liturgy of Domestic Church Life and give you a way to assess your family's strengths and areas for growth. Rate your family on a scale of 1 ("We don't do this at all") to 5 ("This describes us perfectly!").

How Can Families Live the Rite of Christian Relationship?

Through the Rite of Christian Relationship, Catholic families live the priestly mission of their baptism by practicing the sacrificial love that comes from God's heart. Although every family is different, there are some things every family can do to live this rite in full.

___a. We prioritize family time. Because we can only form godly kids if we spend meaningful time together every day, we don't let outside activities compete with our efforts to create a close-knit, family team.

___b. We are extravagantly affectionate. Christ's love is generous and incarnate. As a Christian household, we imitate Christ by being generously and appropriately affectionate, affirming, and supportive of one another.

___c. Pope Saint John Paul II said that Christian relationships are characterized by "mutual self-giving." We work hard to respond to each other's needs (parents and kids) promptly, generously, consistently, and cheerfully.

___d. We practice discipleship discipline in our home. As Saint John Bosco taught, we reject harsh punishments and focus on teaching, supporting, and encouraging godly behavior through "reason, religion, and loving-kindness."

Just imagine how millions of families practicing the above habits could change the world by conveying a truly beautiful, intimate vision of family life. That is the priestly fruit of the Liturgy of Domestic Church Life.

How Can Families Live the Rite of Family Rituals?

Through the Rite of Family Rituals, Catholic families live the prophetic mission of baptism by developing strong family rituals that model Christian attitudes toward work, leisure, relationships, and prayer. Although every family is different, there are some things every family can do to live this rite in full.

___a. Work rituals. Each day, instead of dividing and conquering, we make time to do at least some household chores together. We don't think of chores as just "things that have to get done." We know they are opportunities to learn to be a team and take good care of one another.

___b. Play rituals. Every day, we make a point to play together, enjoy one another's company, and model healthy ways to celebrate our life together.

___c. Talk rituals. Several times a week, we have meaningful conversations (not lectures) about faith, values, how God is showing up for us, and how we can take better care of one another.

___d. Prayer rituals. We pray together as a family throughout each day. We relate to Jesus as another member of our family. We regularly praise him and ask for his help.

Imagine the difference millions of families who dedicated themselves to modeling an authentic Christian approach to work, play, relationships, and God would make. That is the prophetic fruit of the Liturgy of Domestic Church Life.

How Can Families Live the Rite of Reaching Out?

Through the Rite of Reaching Out, Catholic families live the royal mission of their baptism by cultivating a spirit of loving service inside and outside the home. Although it's important to find ways to serve your parish or community together as a family, true Christian service begins at home and extends outward. Every family is different, but there are some things every family can do to live this rite in full.

___a. We take good care of one another at home. Authentic Christian service begins with caring generously for the people under our roof.

___b. We think about others even when we're home. As a family, we donate our gently used items, look for ways to help our neighbors, and make our home a place where others can enjoy godly fun and fellowship.

___c. We are kind, thoughtful, and use good manners in and outside our home. As a family, we're conscious of leaving people happier than we found them.

___d. We regularly engage in charitable service together as a family.

Imagine the impact of millions of Catholic families intentionally looking for ways to cheerfully serve one another and work together to make a positive difference in their parishes and communities. That is the royal fruit of the Liturgy of Domestic Church Life.

How'd You Do?
Every family has its own strengths and areas for growth. Use this quiz to guide discussions in your family about what you're doing well and what you'd like to work on next. The more you live out the Liturgy of Domestic Church Life, the easier it will be for your family to get a clear picture of both your family mission and charism as well.

In on the Secret
So now you're in our not-so-little secret. *Parenting with Grace* isn't really a parenting book at all. At least not the way most people think about par-

enting books. It is meant to be a guide to encountering God's love more fully in your home and changing the world through the ministry of parenting. If you would like more support in learning how to celebrate the Liturgy of Domestic Church Life, we invite you to learn more about our program the CatholicHŌM (Households on Mission) at CatholicHom. org. You can also join our discussion group on Facebook called Catholic-HŌM — Family Discipleship.

As you apply our suggestions and discern the best way to celebrate the Liturgy of Domestic Church Life in your family, we pray that God will abundantly bless you and your children. May the Lord lead you, day by day, to a deeper experience of his love flowing through your home. And may the Lord lead you to a greater awareness of the amazing ways he wants to use your family to be a blessing to others through the witness of your lives.

Yours in Christ,
Dr. Greg & Lisa Popcak
Jacob Popcak, MA, and Rachael Isaac, MSW

Need a Hand? Let Us Help!

Dear Reader,

It can be challenging to be a faithful parent, but you don't have to go it alone. If you find yourself struggling with personal, emotional, spiritual, or relational problems that make it difficult to be the joyful, peaceful, grace-filled person or parent you long to be, we are here to help you on your journey.

Since 1999, the Pastoral Solutions Institute (www.CatholicCounselors.com) has offered Catholic-integrated telecounseling services for Catholic individuals, couples, and families around the world. All of our therapists are fully licensed, have additional training in pastoral theology, and are completely faithful to the teachings of the Church.

We combine the best techniques counseling psychology has to offer with the timeless wisdom of our Catholic faith to help you heal your wounds and achieve your goals. To learn more about how we can help you, visit us online at CatholicCounselors.com. We look forward to helping you take the next step on your journey toward a more abundant marriage, family, or personal life.

Sincerely,
Dr. Greg Popcak
Executive Director
Pastoral Solutions Institute
www.CatholicCounselors.com

References

Ainsworth, Mary D. Salter, Mary C. Blehar, Everett Waters, and Sally N. Wall. *Patterns of Attachment: A Psychological Study of the Strange Situation.* New York: Routledge, 2015.

Bartkus, Justin, and Christian Smith. "A Report on American Catholic Religious Parenting." Notre Dame, IN: McGrath Institute for Church Life, 2015.

Bengtson, Vern L. *Families and Faith: How Religion Is Passed Down across Generations.* Oxford: Oxford University Press, 2017.

Bengtson, Vern L., R. David Hayward, Phil Zuckerman, and Merril Silverstein. "Bringing Up Nones: Intergenerational Influences and Cohort Trends." *Journal for the Scientific Study of Religion* 57(2): June 2018.

Bowlby, John. *A Secure Base: Parent-Child Attachment and Healthy Human Development.* New York: Basic Books, 1999.

Cameron-Smith, Kim. *Discipleship Parenting: Planting the Seeds of Faith.* Huntington, IN: OSV, 2019.

Clinton, Tim, and Gary Sibcy. *Attachments: Why You Love, Feel, and Act the Way You Do.* Nashville: Thomas Nelson, 2009.

Clinton, Tim, and Joshua Straub. *God Attachment: Why You Believe, Act, and Feel the Way You Do about God.* Brentwood, TN: Howard Books, 2014.

Cozolino, Louis. *The Neuroscience of Human Relationships: Attachment and the Developing Social Brain.* New York: W. W. Norton & Co., 2014.

Dwyer, Carol, Carol Dweck, and Heather Carlson-Jaquez. "Using Praise to Enhance Student Resilience and Learning Outcomes." American

Psychological Association, 2010. https://www.apa.org/education
/k12/using-praise.

Egalite, Anna J. "How Family Background Influences Student Achievement." *Education Next* 16, no. 2 (February 17, 2016).

Fiese, Barbara H. *Family Routines and Rituals*. New Haven, CT: Yale University Press, 2006.

Fowler, James W. *Stages of Faith: The Psychology of Human Development and the Quest for Meaning*. New York: HarperOne, 1995.

Gengler, Colleen. Rev. by Jodi Dworkin. "Teens and family meals." University of Minnesota Extension. Accessed December 1, 2020, https://extension.umn.edu/communication-and-screen-time/teens-and-family-meals.

Grabowski, John and Claire. *Raising Catholic Kids for Their Vocations*. Charlotte, NC: Tan, 2019.

Harris, Judith Rich. *The Nurture Assumption: Why Children Turn Out the Way They Do*. Revised and updated. New York: Free Press, 2009.

Hart, Jonathan, Alicia Limke, and Phillip R. Budd. "Attachment and Faith Development." *Journal of Psychology and Theology* 36, no. 2 (2010).

Jerrim, John, Luis Alejandro Lopez-Agudo, and Oscar D. Marcenaro-Gutierrez. "Does It Matter What Children Read? New Evidence Using Longitudinal Census Data from Spain." *Oxford Review of Education* 46, no. 5 (February 27, 2020).

Lam, Chun Bun, Susan M. McHale, and Ann C. Crouter. "Parent-Child Shared Time from Middle Childhood to Late Adolescence: Developmental Course and Adjustment Correlates." *Child Development* 83, no. 6 (2012).

Lehrer, Jonah. "Do Parents Matter?" *Scientific American*, April 9, 2009. https://www.scientificamerican.com/article/parents-peers-children/#.

Lisitsa, Ellie. "An Introduction to the Gottman Method of Relationship Therapy." The Gottman Institute, May 31, 2013. https://www.gottman.com/blog/an-introduction-to-the-gottman-method-of-relationship-therapy/.

Maselko, J., L. Kubzansky, L. Lipsitt, and S. L. Buka. "Mother's Affection at 8 Months Predicts Emotional Distress in Adulthood." *Journal of Epidemiology and Community Health* 65, no. 7 (2011).

Maslach, Christina, and Michael P. Leiter. "Understanding the Burnout Experience: Recent Research and Its Implications for Psychiatry." *World Psychiatry* 15, no. 2 (June 2016): 103–11.

Mayo Clinic Staff. "Chronic Stress Puts Your Health at Risk." Healthy Lifestyle: Stress Management, March 19, 2019. https://www .mayoclinic.org/healthy-lifestyle/stress-management/in-depth /stress/art-20046037.

Meier, Ann, and Kelly Musick. "Variation in Associations Between Family Dinners and Adolescent Well-Being." *Journal of Marriage and Family* 76, no. 1 (2014).

Mendelsohn, Alan, Carolyn Brockmeyer Cates, Adriana Weisleder, Samantha Berkule Johnson, Anne M. Seery, Caitlin F. Canfield, Harris S. Huberman, and Benard P. Dreyer. "Reading Aloud, Play, and Social-Emotional Development." *Pediatrics* 141, no. 5 (May 2018).

Milkie, Melissa A., Kei M. Nomaguchi, and Kathleen E. Denny. "Does the Amount of Time Mothers Spend with Children or Adolescents Matter?" *Journal of Marriage and Family* 77, no. 2 (2015).

Narváez, Darcia. *Neurobiology and the Development of Human Morality: Evolution, Culture, and Wisdom.* New York: W. W. Norton & Co., 2014.

Neufeld, Gordon, and Gabor Maté. *Hold On to Your Kids: Why Parents Need to Matter More Than Peers.* New York: Ballantine Books, 2006.

Oldfield, Jeremy, Neil Humphrey, and Judith Hebron. "The Role of Parental and Peer Attachment Relationships and School Connectedness in Predicting Adolescent Mental Health Outcomes." *Child and Adolescent Mental Health* 21, no. 1 (May 18, 2015): 21–29.

Oliner, Samuel P., and Pearl M. Oliner. *The Altruistic Personality: Rescuers of Jews in Nazi Europe.* New York: Touchstone, 1992.

Osewska, Elżbieta, and Barbara Simonič. "A Civilization of Love according to John Paul II." *The Person and the Challenges* 9, no. 1 (2019): 23–32.

Ouellet, Marc Cardinal. *Divine Likeness: Toward a Trinitarian Anthropology of the Family.* Grand Rapids, MI: Eerdmans, 2006.

Partnership to End Addiction. "The Importance of Family Dinners 2012," September 2012. https://drugfree.org/reports/the -importance-of-family-dinners-viii/

Shivanandan, Mary. *The Holy Family: Model Not Exception*. Glen Echo, MD: KM Associates, 2018.

Siegel, Daniel J. MD, and Tina Payne Bryson, PhD. *The Power of Showing Up: How Parental Presence Shapes Who Our Kids Become and How Their Brains Get Wired*. New York: Ballantine Books, 2020.

Siegel, Daniel J. *Pocket Guide to Interpersonal Neurobiology: An Integrative Handbook of the Mind*. New York: W. W. Norton, 2012.

Society for Consumer Psychology. "A New Strategy to Alleviate Sadness: Bring the Emotion to Life: Researchers Show How Characters from the Movie 'Inside Out' Hold the Key to Regulating Emotions and Behavior." ScienceDaily.com, October 3, 2019. https://www .sciencedaily.com/releases/2019/10/191003103515.htm.

US Bureau of Labor Statistics. "Average Hours Per Day Parents Spent Caring for and Helping Household Children as Their Main Activity." American Time Use Survey, accessed November 24, 2020. https://www.bls.gov/charts/american-time-use/activity-by-parent .htm.

Yoshida, Sachine, Yoshihiro Kawahara, Takuya Sasatani, Ken Kiyono, Yo Kobayashi, and Hiromasa Funato. "Infants Show Physiological Responses Specific to Parental Hugs." iScience, April 24, 2020.

Notes

Chapter 2

1. Pope Saint John Paul II, Homily, January 28, 1979, Vatican.va.

2. Marc Cardinal Ouellet, *Divine Likeness: Toward a Trinitarian Anthropology of the Family* (Grand Rapids, MI: Eerdmans, 2006).

Chapter 3

1. Pope Francis, *Amoris Laetitia*, accessed December 20, 2020, Vatican.va, par. 87.

2. Chun Bun Lam, Susan M. McHale, and Ann C. Crouter, "Parent-Child Shared Time from Middle Childhood to Late Adolescence: Developmental Course and Adjustment Correlates," *Child Development* 83, no. 6 (2012): 2089–103.

3. Melissa A. Milkie, Kei M. Nomaguchi, and Kathleen E. Denny, "Does the Amount of Time Mothers Spend With Children or Adolescents Matter?" *Journal of Marriage and Family* 77, no. 2 (2015): 355–72.

4. Barbara H. Fiese, *Family Routines and Rituals* (New Haven, CT: Yale University Press, 2006).

5. Elise Harris, "Eat with Your Family, Not with Your Smartphone, Pope Says," Catholic News Agency, November 11, 2015.

6. Charlie Plain, "Project EAT Study Shows It's Never Too Late to Benefit from Family Meals," University of Minnesota School of Public Health, October 25, 2017, https://www.sph.umn.edu/news /parents-can-experience-health-benefits-eating-family-meals/; Ann Meier and Kelly Musick, "Variation in Associations Between Family Dinners and Adolescent Well-Being," *Journal of Marriage and Family*

76, no. 1 (2014): 13–23; Partnership to End Addiction, "The Importance of Family Dinners 2012," September 2012, https://drugfree.org/reports/the-importance-of-family-dinners-viii/.

7. "This likeness reveals that man, who is the only creature on earth which God willed for itself, cannot fully find himself except through a sincere gift of himself." Pastoral Constitution on the Church in the Modern World, *Gaudium et Spes,* accessed December 20, 2020, Vatican.va, par. 24.

8. Daniel J. Siegel, MD, and Tina Payne Bryson, PhD, *The Power of Showing Up: How Parental Presence Shapes Who Our Kids Become and How Their Brains Get Wired* (New York: Ballantine Books, 2020).

9. Sachine Yoshida, Yoshihiro Kawahara, Takuya Sasatani, Ken Kiyono, Yo Kobayashi, and Hiromasa Funato, "Infants Show Physiological Responses Specific to Parental Hugs," *iScience* 23, no. 4 (April 24, 2020).

Chapter 4

1. Pope Saint John Paul II, *Familiaris Consortio,* accessed December 20, 2020, Vatican.va, par. 17.

2. Visit Momfidence.org to learn more.

3. Vern L. Bengtson, *Families and Faith: How Religion Is Passed Down across Generations* (Oxford: Oxford University Press, 2017); Darcia Narváez, *Neurobiology and the Development of Human Morality: Evolution, Culture, and Wisdom* (New York: W. W. Norton & Co., 2014).

4. Pope Francis tweet, October 27, 2015.

Chapter 5

1. Mary Shivanandan, *The Holy Family: Model Not Exception* (Glen Echo, MD: KM Associates, 2018).

Chapter 6

1. Elżbieta Osewska and Barbara Simonič, "A Civilization of Love according to John Paul II," *The Person and the Challenges* 9, no. 1 (2019): 23–32.

Chapter 7

1. Narváez, *Neurobiology and the Development of Human Morality*; Fiese, *Family Routines and Rituals*; Vern L. Bengtson, R. David Hayward, Phil Zuckerman, and Merril Silverstein, "Bringing Up Nones: Intergenerational Influences and Cohort Trends," *Journal for the Scientific Study of Religion* 57, no. 2 (June 2018).

2. Matt Hadro, "Why Catholics Are Leaving the Faith by Age 10—And What Parents Can Do About It," Catholic News Agency, December 17, 2016, https://www.catholicnewsagency.com/news/why -catholics-are-leaving-the-faith-by-age-10-and-what-parents-can-do -about-it-48918.

3. Bengtson, *Families and Faith*; Justin Bartkus and Christian Smith, *A Report on American Catholic Religious Parenting* (Notre Dame, IN: McGrath Institute for Church Life, 2015).

4. Gordon Neufeld and Gabor Maté, *Hold On to Your Kids: Why Parents Need to Matter More Than Peers* (New York: Ballantine Books, 2006); Jeremy Oldfield, Neil Humphrey, and Judith Hebron, "The Role of Parental and Peer Attachment Relationships and School Connectedness in Predicting Adolescent Mental Health Outcomes," *Child and Adolescent Mental Health* 21, no. 1 (May 18, 2015): 21–29.

5. John Bowlby, *A Secure Base: Parent-Child Attachment and Healthy Human Development* (New York: Basic Books, 1999); Mary D. Salter Ainsworth, Mary C. Blehar, Everett Waters, and Sally N. Wall, *Patterns of Attachment: A Psychological Study of the Strange Situation* (New York: Routledge, 2015).

6. Pope John Paul II, *Evangelium Vitae*, accessed December 20, 2020, Vatican.va, par. 93.

7. Louis Cozolino, *The Neuroscience of Human Relationships: Attachment and the Developing Social Brain* (New York: W. W. Norton, 2014); Narváez, *Neurobiology and the Development of Human Morality*.

8. Daniel J. Siegel, *Pocket Guide to Interpersonal Neurobiology: An Integrative Handbook of the Mind* (New York: W. W. Norton, 2012).

9. Dr. Tim Clinton and Dr. Gary Sibcy, *Attachments: Why You Love, Feel, and Act the Way You Do* (Nashville: Thomas Nelson,

2009); Dr. Tim Clinton and Dr. Joshua Straub, *God Attachment: Why You Believe, Act, and Feel the Way You Do about God* (Brentwood, TN: Howard Books, 2014).

Chapter 8

1. James W. Fowler, *Stages of Faith: The Psychology of Human Development and the Quest for Meaning* (New York: HarperOne, 1995); Narváez, *Neurobiology and the Development of Human Morality.*

Chapter 9

1. Bishop Robert Barron, "Priests, Prophets, Kings," *Word on Fire*, February 14, 2014, https://www.wordonfire.org/resources/article/priests-prophets-kings/477/.

2. Christina Maslach and Michael P. Lieter, "Understanding the Burnout Experience: Recent Research and Its Implications for Psychiatry," *World Psychiatry* 15, no. 2 (June 2016): 103–111.

3. Society for Consumer Psychology, "A New Strategy to Alleviate Sadness: Bring the Emotion to Life," ScienceDaily.com, October 3, 2019, https://www.sciencedaily.com/releases/2019/10/191003103515.htm.

Chapter 10

1. Cozolino, *The Neuroscience of Human Relationships*; Narváez, *Neurobiology and the Development of Human Morality.*

Part 3

1. Samuel P. Oliner and Pearl M. Oliner, *The Altruistic Personality: Rescuers of Jews in Nazi Europe* (New York: Touchstone, 1992).

Chapter 14

1. Carol Dwyer, Carol Dweck, and Heather Carlson-Jaquez, "Using Praise to Enhance Student Resilience and Learning Outcomes," American Psychological Association, 2010, https://www.apa.org/education/k12/using-praise.

Chapter 18

1. Ellie Lisitsa, "An Introduction to the Gottman Method of Relationship Therapy," The Gottman Institute, May 31, 2013, https://www.gottman.com/blog/an-introduction-to-the-gottman-method-of-relationship-therapy/.

Chapter 23

1. Fiese, *Family Routines and Rituals*.

2. Bartkus, in Gregory K. Popcak, ed., *Renewing Catholic Family Life: Experts Explore New Directions in Family Spirituality and Family Ministry* (Huntington, IN: Our Sunday Visitor, 2020).

3. Benedict XVI, *Deus Caritas Est*, accessed December 20, 2020, Vatican.va, par. 5.

About the Authors

Dr. Greg and Lisa Popcak are the authors of more than twenty books and the hosts of More2Life, a call-in advice program airing weekdays on EWTN and SiriusXM 130. Together, they direct CatholicCounselors. com, a Catholic telecounseling practice serving couples, families, and individuals around the world. In collaboration with Holy Cross Family Ministries, Dr. Greg and Lisa founded the Peyton Institute for Domestic Church Life, which promotes family spirituality and family well-being through professional trainings and original research. The Popcaks are members of the US Conference of Catholic Bishops' National Advisory Board for Marriage and Family Ministry.

ALSO AVAILABLE FROM OSV

FOR PARENTS

Parenting Your Kids with Grace (Birth to Age 10)
Dr. Greg and Lisa Popcak
Family therapist and parent Gregory Popcak and his wife, Lisa, are back with *Parenting Your Kids with Grace (Birth to Age 10)*. Building on their best-selling book *Parenting with Grace*, first published twenty years ago, this new volume draws on the same parenting principles and provides up-to-date research to guide parents through each stage of child development from birth to age ten.

Talking to Youth About Sexuality: A Parents' Guide
Fr. Kris Stubna and Mike Aquilina worked with parents, doctors, educators, and catechists to develop a practical resource for answering questions and encouraging meaningful conversations with your child.

Discipleship Parenting: Planting the Seeds of Faith
Learn to get past the obstacles to raising faithful Catholic children, and till the soil of their little hearts so the word of God can take root and grow. Learn about the seven ideal growing conditions and how to cultivate them in your home: love, balance, play, merciful discipline, empathy, radiant faith, and a strong marriage.

Available at OSVCatholicBookstore.com or wherever books are sold.

**The Tech Talk: Strategies for Families
in a Digital World**
Author Michael Horne, a Catholic parent and clinical
psychologist, knows all too well the struggles families face
understanding and dealing with how technology impacts
our lives. In *The Tech Talk*, he zeroes in on the dangers of
children's unsupervised forays into the digital world, shows
you what's out there, and includes strategies for keeping it all
in balance.

FOR TEENS AND TWEENS

Be Yourself! A Journal for Catholic Girls
Packed with beautiful artwork, quizzes, journaling questions,
inspirational quotes from seven female saints, and passages
from the Catechism of the Catholic Church and Scripture,
the Be Yourself! journal is a fun way to help girls become the
women God created them to be. Ages 9 and up.
Be Yourself: A Journal for Catholic Boys
Be Yourself: A Journal for Catholic Boys was designed for
boys to understand their identity and individuality, with the
help of their Catholic faith. Packed full of great art, quizzes,
journaling questions, quotes from the saints, Scripture
verses, and passages from the Catechism of the Catholic
Church, the Be Yourself journal helps boys become the men
God created them to be.

way | truth | life, New Testament (NABRE)
Just for teens and young adults, this New Testament (NABRE) is an invitation — to know Christ, the way, the truth, and the life, through his Word. It is also delightfully designed with vibrant images that invite readers to linger and encourage reflection and prayer. Includes 21 original essays by young adults share how God has touched their lives through Scripture.

The Adventure: Living Out Your Relationship with God (Catholic Edition)
A one-of-a-kind guide to the adventure God is calling you to live. It includes getting to know God, why having a relationship with him matters, and how to become friends with him (yes, it's possible). You'll learn how he talks to you, how you can talk to him, how you can do things with him, and how we connect with him and one another through the sacraments and the Church.

Road Signs for Catholic Teens
Getting the keys to the family car has been a symbol of independence ever since there were cars. You're not a kid anymore, and you can make your own choices — speed, route, direction, destination. That's a lot like your spiritual life. You can take the wheel of your faith, get out there, and go. And just like a good road trip, your spiritual life can be full of adventure, joy, and exhilaration. But there are also signs to watch out for and hazards to avoid.

Available at OSVCatholicBookstore.com or wherever books are sold.